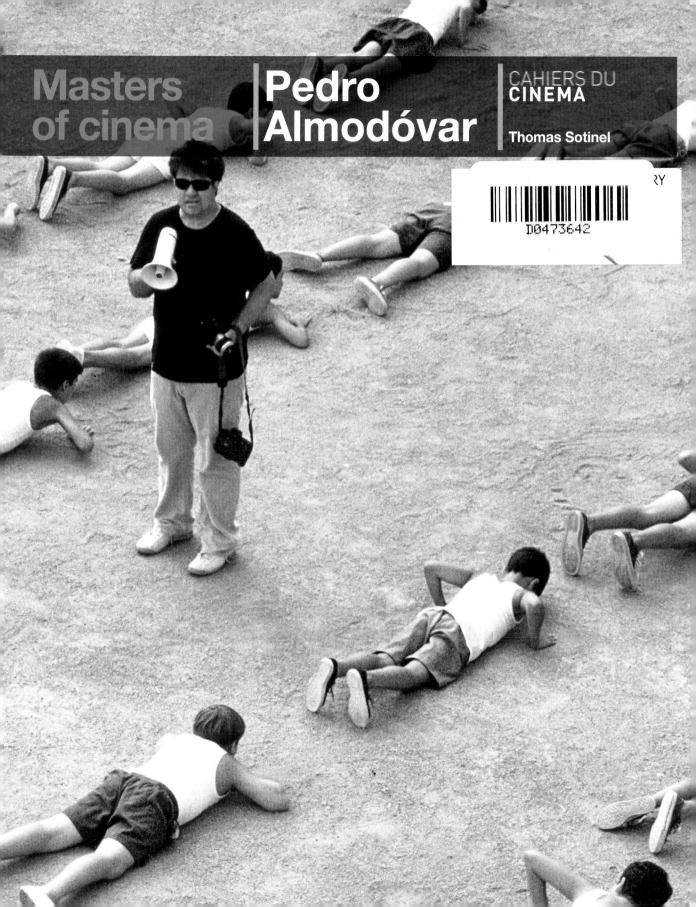

Masters
of cinema

Pedro
Almodóvar

CAHIERS DU
CINEMA

Thomas Sotinel

Contents

Pedro Almodóvar in 1991.

Ix I/17

Introduction

Acknowledged by film critics and historians and adored by a wide and loyal public ever since the success of *Women on the Verge of a Nervous Breakdown* in 1988, Pedro Almodóvar has taken his place in the film directors' Hall of Fame. At first glance, he has the appearance of a true heir of Bergman and Fellini: a white-haired, patriarchal figure who amasses honorary degrees and whose films are eagerly awaited all over the world. And yet Almodóvar is not an intellectual; his father was a mule-driver from La Mancha, and while he was working for the Spanish telephone company Telefónica he taught himself about cinema without the help of any film institute or university. Nor did he spring fully formed onto the international cinema scene. When he came to the world's notice, in the early 1980s, it was as a leading figure in the Madrid 'Movida', the cultural revolution that followed Franco's death in 1975.

Collecting awards and wooed by Hollywood, this emblem of Spain's opening up to the world's cultural movements could easily have become a director on the international scene. Instead, he has remained entirely Spanish, shooting increasingly sophisticated stories in Castille and La Mancha and creating among his compatriots a mixture of admiration and exasperation that makes him, even today, the object of fierce controversy.

Almodóvar the man remains a mystery: both reserved and exhibitionistic, a patriarch who retains eternal youth, an international star who is also provincial. His work, on the other hand, has a luminous coherence: from the joyful transgressions of *Pepi, Luci, Bom and Other Girls on the Heap* to the pervading melancholy of *Broken Embraces* we find the same pleasure in enabling the audience to share the director's power. You have to be a filmmaker to delight in your ability to subject people and things to the only law that counts, that which provides the title of one of Almodóvar's most beautiful films: *The Law of Desire*.

Marisa Paredes and Cecilia Roth in *All About my Mother* (1999).   5

A Man of La Mancha

Pepi, Luci, Bom and Other Girls on the Heap

Pedro Almodóvar as a young man in the 1970s.

Right: Pedro Almodóvar and his mother, Francesca Caballero, in the 1950s.

The mule-driver's son

Up until the early 1990s, Pedro Almodóvar was said to have been born in Calzada de Calatrava, in La Mancha, on 25 September 1949. Later, the calendar shed a couple of years, although the day didn't change, and the son of Antonio Almodóvar and Francesca 'Paca' Caballero came into the world in 1951, or even 1952. That perhaps suggests a touch of the flirt, but it should also ring an initial warning bell: Almodóvar's real life is beyond our grasp. We shall see no more than our hero wishes to show us, and as the years and the films unfold we'll discover that his life is so tightly woven into his fiction that it's impossible to disentangle the threads of this complex tapestry.

We're in La Mancha, then, a decade or so after the end of the Spanish Civil War. The country is poor and backward, and the surrounding region even more so. Generalissimo Francisco Franco had seized absolute power, and as early as 1944 he knew that his prudent posture of neutrality during World War II would protect him from the fate meted out to Hitler and Mussolini, his allies in the Civil War. Having been put in power by the Fascists and the Nazis, he was maintained there by the United States, which would soon lavish on Spain the benefits of its patronage. This turnaround provided the theme for a film which showed that *franquismo* did not extinguish all forms of creativity or stifle every critical spirit: Luis Berlanga's *Bienvenido Mister Marshall!* (*Welcome, Mr Marshall!*), released in 1952.

Berlanga, then aged thirty-two, was one of the few directors of the period who could make films of any interest without falling foul of the censors, but in general the intellectual and cultural situation was, like the economy, grim. In the cinema, you could see Hollywood films and sentimental Spanish productions. Josélito, the child singer with the golden voice, came to fame in 1956. At the time, this meant nothing to the Almodóvar family, because Calzada de Calatrava had no cinema. Pedro was Antonio's and Francesca's third child. He had two older sisters, Antonia and María Jesús, and Agustín, his younger brother, who was to become his producer, was born a few years after him.

According to the writer Juan José Millás, who studied the family tree in connection with an article he wrote for *El País* during the shooting of *Volver* (2006), Antonio Almodóvar was the last of a long line of mule-drivers engaged in transporting wine from Calzada de Calatrava to El Centenillo, a small Andalucian town about fifty kilometres away. In the first half of the twentieth century, when Spain's poor road network was notorious throughout Europe, business was good enough for Pedro's grandfather to own a winery on Calle General Aguilera, the same street on which Francesca Caballero, Antonio's future wife and Pedro's mother, was born.

By the 1960s, road-building and the increasing use of motor vehicles dealt a fatal blow to the last of the mule-drivers, including Antonio Almodóvar. The family had to leave Calzada de Calatrava and move to Orellana la Vieja, in Extremadura. Pedro was only eight years old at the time, but he has always been proud of his 'Manchego' identity. At first, he saw it as a burden. In his early interviews, he could not speak harshly enough of the place where he was born: 'Down there, life's meaningless, it's a region where people don't work for the pleasure of it. If you have money, you don't use it to enjoy life, but to buy more and more land. The austerity's horrible,' he told the newspaper *ABC* in 1986. In a book about Almodóvar by the critic Nuria Vidal, published in 1988, he returns to this theme in a more poetic mood: 'To me, the image of a Manchego is of a man whose only mirror is the water in his well. In La Mancha, there used to be, and still are, many suicides. People hang themselves or throw themselves down a well.'

It is not until Almodóvar's fourth film, *What Have I Done to Deserve This?* (1984), that the idea of returning to one's village becomes one of redemption, in a humorous vein; Almodóvar then makes it a central theme, one that appears in *Tie Me Up! Tie Me Down!* (1990) and *The Flower of My Secret* (1995) and is developed fully in *Volver.*

The good fathers

In Orellana la Vieja, Almodóvar and his family lived in a very poor neighbourhood. Francesca Caballero opened 'a business involving reading and writing letters, just like in the film *Central do Brasil*'. That's how the director described it in 1999, the day after his mother died, at a time when Walter Salles's film, to which he was referring, was enjoying great success. Paca used the services of her son, a good student, and he noticed the way she embellished the letters she read, to match the recipients' expectations. In the same text, Almodóvar explains that this process showed him 'how reality needs fiction in order to be complete, to be pleasanter, more tolerable'.

A short film presented live by the director himself in the 1970s.

When Pedro was about ten years old, some kind soul drew the parish priest's attention to this gifted child. That planted the idea of making him a priest. In Spain at that time, a religious vocation still offered a means of social advancement for the most underprivileged, and Pedro's parents agreed to send him to the Salesian Fathers at Cáceres, in Extremadura. 'To me, Cáceres in the Sixties was like Paris in the Seventies,' Almodóvar told F. B. Boquerini, a critic who published a book about him in 1989. While he was with the Salesians, Almodóvar sang solo with the children's choir, lost his faith sometime between the ages of ten and twelve and witnessed the sexual abuse that he put into his film *Bad Education* (2004). As he said to Nuria Vidal: 'Life didn't make sense, you didn't know why you'd been put there, the only genuine thing was the boredom.' And on paedophilia he had this to say: 'It was a source of pain, because you should discover sex naturally, not brutally. For two or three years I couldn't be left by myself, out of pure fear.'

In 1983, he told the following story to the now defunct *Diario 16*, following the release of *Dark Habits* (1983): 'The Father Superior of the boarding school where I was a pupil was very fond of the song *Come Back to Sorrento*. At the time, I was a soloist in the choir ... One of the priests had the idea of giving the Father Superior a version of *Come Back to Sorrento* for a name-day gift, with new words ... that went: "Gardener, gardener, among the flowers all day, protecting their scent with the flame of your love." What followed was even more ambiguous. We boys ate in one refectory and the priests in another. During the meal, someone took me out and brought me to the priests. They had had a bit to drink and had undone a few buttons on their cassocks They stood me in the middle and without further ado, I sang to the Father Superior his favourite song, with the new words in which he was a gardener and the boys were flowers that he amorously cultivated with the flame of his love.'

It was at this time, too, around 1960, that Almodóvar had his first encounter with cinema. His brother Agustín recalls that Pedro would take him to see films, that he bought the magazine *Fotogramas* and collected photos of actresses. When he got home, Pedro would tell the stories of the films to his sisters, reinventing them all the time.

Franco? Who he?

There is an empty space at the centre of Pedro Almodóvar's cinema – the absence of any memory of the Spanish Civil War and the man who won it, General Francisco Franco.

Early on in his career, Almodóvar would often say that the best way to obliterate the legacy of the Caudillo, who held the country in the grip of his cruel paternalism until his death in 1975 (when Almodóvar was twenty-five) was to ignore it.

Of his films, only *Matador* (1986) can be seen partly as a metaphor for the conflict between the two Spains: one secular and progressive, represented in their different ways by Assumpta Serna and Chus Lampreave; the other steeped in religion and bullfighting and embodied in the performances of Nacho Martínez, as the bullfighter, and Julieta Serrano,

as the devotee of Opus Dei. While never dealing directly with politics, Almodóvar's films are firmly rooted in the times in which they were made. The flashbacks to the characters' childhood are clearly set in the period – clothes and furniture are authentic – but History does not obtrude. There is perhaps one exception: the prologue to *Live Flesh* (1997), which shows Victor's birth on a Madrid bus, on the very night a state of emergency is declared.

By showing how the authorities take advantage of this happy event to distract public attention, Almodóvar reveals that he was an alert viewer of 'No-Do', or *Noticiera Documental*, the newsreel that the regime decreed had to be shown during every cinema programme.

By contrast, the sequences in *Bad Education* that are set in

the 1960s take the social and political context for granted; we only guess at the background of intellectual and moral poverty in which the priests' domination over their pupils flourishes. This does not mean Almodóvar is unaware of the history of his country. There are constant references to current developments, from the bewilderment of the police officer in *Pepi, Luci, Bom and Other Girls on the Heap* (1980) to the changes in prison conditions that we see reflected in Benigno's treatment in *Talk to Her* (2002).

Over the years we've seen Victoria Abril in *High Heels* (1991) burst out laughing as she announces an ETA bombing on TV, and Marisa Paredes in *The Flower of My Secret*, weeping for her soldier husband who has gone to fight in Bosnia.

In his role as a citizen, Almodóvar takes an active part in debate, especially when it involves his profession. He originally defended the system of government funding for film production, set up in 1983 by the government of Felipe González, only to attack it a few years later for having become ossified. When José María Aznar came to power, Almodóvar became a constant critic of his foreign and cultural policies, and in 2003 he took part in a demonstration against the American invasion of Iraq. (He had also demonstrated against Basque terrorism.)

The day after the Madrid train bombings of 11 March 2004 he went as far as to accuse Aznar's Partido Popular of attempting to carry out a *coup d'état*, and had to make a public apology.

Opposite page: the sleeve of *Satanasa* (1983), one of the disks recorded by Pedro Almodóvar and Fanny McNamara.

Below: Pedro and Agustín Almodóvar, looking at a poster of Marilyn Monroe in 1975.

City lights and footlights

By 1967, the boarder with the Salesian Fathers had long since rejected the priesthood. With his school-leaving certificate in his pocket, he announced to his family that he had decided to leave La Mancha for Madrid, where his sister María Jesús, who had married a member of the Civil Guard, was living. He had a row with his father, who in the end let him go. Pedro left for the big city and lived for a while with his sister. He soon headed for Paris and London, where he thought of settling, but returned to Spain. He had let his hair grow, and was hired as an extra in films that needed lots of hippies for crowd scenes. He sold 'flower power' accessories in the street, and made a trip to Ibiza. But none of this really suited him and in 1969, after doing his military service in the air force, he got an administrative job with Telefónica.

The national telecommunications company was going through a phase of rapid development, as Spain began to catch up with the rest of Europe in technology, but it was still one of those typical European bureaucracies in which members of the lower middle class found their natural level. The steady salaries such enterprises paid enabled rural workers to move to the city, and by demanding no

Pedro Almodóvar on the set of *Pepi, Luci, Bom and Other Girls on the Heap* (1980).

more than the bare minimum of time-keeping and effort, Telefónica also gave its most creative employees the leisure in which to cultivate their talents. Almodóvar stayed there twelve years, and did not give up his day job until 1982, after the release of *Labyrinth of Passion*.

In 1972, Agustín, who was the first member of his family to go to university — he studied chemical engineering — joined Pedro in Madrid. He described that time to Nuria Vidal: 'The people he knew seemed very cool. Pedro knew people who smoked joints and listened to David Bowie, who was completely unknown at that time. It was a circle of intimate friends, which didn't open up easily,

because the situation was so tightly controlled.' The fact is, Spain was still a dictatorship. Pedro could probably have got a place at the film school, but the government had closed it down in 1971 and it didn't reopen until after Franco's death. In any case, he would have made a much worse student than he did a self-taught practitioner.

The 'Movida'

In Madrid, Almodóvar read, listened to music and, above all, was a regular visitor to the first cinemas to show experimental films, which were just then opening up. In 1974, he got hold of a Super 8 camera and started making films. Right from the start, what mattered to him was telling stories. His shorts made in Super 8 are now a matter of legend. They have not been shown for almost twenty years, and the only way we can get even a vague idea of what they were like is by reading the synopses. The first one, *Two Whores, or, A Love Story that Ends in Marriage* (1974), already features lovers who exchange their roles, their sex and their points of view. Like those that followed, it was made over a period of time, depending on the availability of friends and the money required to buy film. Almodóvar has often said that at that time he had no thought of becoming a director whose films would be shown in cinemas, but at the same time he didn't reckon on keeping these first essays to himself.

Rather than trying to record a synchronous soundtrack, Almodóvar projected his early shorts in person, adding (with Agustín's help) live commentary, sound effects and music. They were thus also performances, and their ephemeral nature is one of the reasons Almodóvar gives for withdrawing them from circulation. In the space of five years he made about a dozen short films, to which he added 'fill-up' material, trailers for imaginary feature films and parodies of advertisements or newsreels.

He encountered an underground theatre group, Los Goliardos, headed by the producer, director and writer Félix Rotaeta. Among the company's actresses was a woman, Carmen Maura, who came from a very good family and was herself a mother, but had no respect for social conventions. Almodóvar played small parts with this group, in Sartre's *Les Mains Sales* and Lorca's *The House of Bernarda Alba*, for example. This experience was helpful to him in preparing the performances that accompanied the showings of his short films. He also hung out with musicians and wasn't shy about going up on stage to sing, although he admits himself that he had lost the fine voice he had as a schoolboy. With his friend Fabio de Miguel, who performs under the name of Fabio (or Fanny) McNamara, he formed a duo in the early 1980s, and recorded several disks.

Almodóvar liked to dress up on stage, mixing together cheap clothes he would buy in department stores, and sometimes (as Juan José Millás reports) borrowing an item of his brother-in-law's Civil Guard uniform. He was at the centre of the ferment that was brewing in Madrid.

Franco died in 1975 and Spain had subsequently embarked on the journey that would bring it ever closer to the rest of Europe. The underground culture of the big cities was coming to the surface, in Barcelona and especially in Madrid. Overnight, the seat of Falangist power turned into a new Babylon whose forte was to be joyfully provocative, with the 'Movida' leading the way. This slang term can be translated as 'party' or 'rave', and while it lasted, Madrid enjoyed a few years (generally considered to have coincided with the tenure of the Socialist Enrique Tierno Galván as mayor of Madrid from 1979 to 1986) of intensively catching up with everything the dictatorship had denied it. Harsh sexual repression disappeared within a few months, a gay scene blossomed and the cinema dubbed 'S', which was more or less pornographic, took over the city's screens. The Movida was both an artistic and a social phenomenon, a mixture of punk and cabaret, and it was led by musicians, like the singer Alaska, designers (Javier Mariscal, for example), theatre groups like Los Goliardos, and a filmmaker, Pedro Almodóvar.

Like every cultural scene at the time — the New York of Jean-Michel Basquiat and Kid Creole, the Paris of Taxi Girl and Alain Pacadis — the Madrid Movida saw the consumption of a lot of hard drugs; they created devastation in Almodóvar's circle, but he was able to avoid their effects. The Telefónica employee was a night-owl, on the go twenty-four hours a day, and it's hard to believe he didn't indulge.

In 1978, Almodóvar said goodbye to the amateur life. He made his first feature film, again using Super 8. Its title, *Folle ... Folle ... Fólleme Tim!* (*Fuck ... Fuck ... Fuck Me, Tim!*) contains a pun on the word *folletín* (soap opera). It tells the story of two blind people, one a guitarist, the other a shop assistant, drawn to each other by desire but driven apart by ambition. This time Almodóvar recorded a soundtrack, and after presenting his film in person on several occasions (the premiere took place in the former residence of the Catalan millionaire and financier of Franco's *coup d'état*, Juan March) he let it fend for itself. In the same year, he switched to 16mm and for the first time worked with professional actors, on *Salome* (1978), a short that combines two stories from the Bible: Abraham's sacrifice of Isaac and the death of John the Baptist. In 1977, Spain's first free national elections brought the 'centrist' 13

Opening credits of *Pepi, Luci, Bom and Other Girls on the Heap* (1980) by the painter Ceesepe.

Guion y
direccion
Pedro
Almodovar

Produccion:
Ester Rambal
Pastora Delgado
Ayte. direccion
M.A. Perez Campos

Una produccion
de
Pepon Corominas
para Figaro
Films

Adolfo Suárez to power. The delights of representative democracy prompted Almodóvar to write the outline for a photo-novel entitled *Erecciones generales* ('General Erections'). Félix Rotaeta and Carmen Maura, his friends from Los Goliardos, persuaded him to turn it into the screenplay of his first real film.

Average girls

Pepi, Luci, Bom y otras chicas del montón (*Pepi, Luci, Bom and Other Girls on the Heap*) took a year to shoot, starting in June 1979. Félix Rotaeta obtained the initial funding, but it was far too little to complete the film. When it finally came out, this was Almodóvar's explanation for the breaks in continuity that punctuate it: 'At the beginning, Pepi (Carmen Maura) goes to open the door to the police officer (Félix Rotaeta) in June 1979; she sits down in the living room in December of the same year, and starts talking to the officer in June 1980. My only concern was to get to the words "The End".'

Carmen Maura still gets emotional when she recalls this epic, haphazard shoot, on which fifteen-hour days would be followed by long interruptions. Some roles were filled at the last minute because the actor they had in mind wasn't available. In the end, it was the producer, Pepón Coromina, who made it possible to finish *Pepi, Luci, Bom*. The film was presented out of competition at the 1980 San Sebastián Film Festival. The festival, which had been set up by Franco as a snub to Cannes and Venice, was changing as fast as the rest of Spain, and it gave this piece of Madrid craziness a warm welcome. As Diego Galán wrote in the recently launched *El País*: 'Few films in the history of Spanish cinema have reached the same level of humour, caustic wit, freedom or freshness as *Pepi, Luci, Bom*.'

Other commentators took the strange film for a satire on the capital's morals. It has to be said that *Pepi, Luci, Bom* is a film that defies strict categorization because it changes as it goes along. As Almodóvar explained in *El País*: 'It's a cop movie because the male character's a police officer thirsting for vengeance. It's a comedy about women because there are lots of lovely, laid-back girls in it. It's a pop film, with its pace, superficiality and cheek, its refusal to be more than it is. And because Alaska y Los Pegamoides are in it, and because it includes adverts and songs. It's also a Bergman film. And a Cukor film (because there are more girls).'

Olvido 'Alaska' Gara in *Pepi, Luci, Bom and Other Girls on the Heap* (1980).

16

At the time, few people would really have thought of mentioning Pedro Almodóvar in the same breath as those great names. Over twenty-five years after its difficult birth, *Pepi,Luci, Bom* still has an exasperating charm that includes elements of both a rough sketch and the delicate illuminations produced by an artist who already knows what he's capable of doing. The characters are very clearly drawn: the smart, ambitious Pepi (Carmen Maura is the director's alter ego here), Luci, who finds happiness in servitude and suffering, and Bom, the doomed artist, who constantly has to be rescued from the dangerous situations she creates for herself. The film is perfectly in tune with its time: the sadistic cop worries that 'with all this democracy you don't know where we're going to end up'. And when we reach the epilogue, and the two friends Pepi and Bom decide to move in together, their comment, 'What a lot of changes in one day!' resonated with Spanish audiences who had seen their country radically transformed within the space of a few months.

A whole tribe of artists and technicians had already formed around Almodóvar. They included the mainstays of his future production team (the editor José 'Pepe' Salcedo, who was to stay with him, and his brother Agustín, who appears briefly on screen), as well as the actresses who made up this changing but loyal company: Carmen Maura, long his favourite, before she was banished and then welcomed back, and the Argentinian Cecilia Roth (seen in the scatological adverts that punctuate the film), who would play the lead in *All About My Mother* (1999) twenty years later.

The film was released on 27 October 1980 at the Alphaville, Madrid's leading art house. It showed continuously for the next three years, and took 40 million pesetas at the box office.

In a 1986 interview with *El País*, Almodóvar, who was now poised to become a major figure in world cinema, looked back at the film: 'It's so full of faults, they're an essential part of its style. And in spite of everything, *Pepi, Luci, Bom and Other Girls on the Heap* contains some of the best sequences I've ever made.' At that time the Madrid night-bird was still working for Telefónica, but so many people shared his judgement, he could now truly be seen as a film director. By the time *Pepi, Luci, Bom and Other Girls on the Heap* came out, he had already started writing his next film.

What Makes a Director?

From *Labyrinth of Passion* to *Law of Desire*

Pedro Almodóvar in 1986.

A film that's also a trailer

Labyrinth of Passion (1982), Almodóvar's second feature film, was still not made strictly according to the rules of commercial cinema. Funding for it came, not from a producer or distributor, but from the owners of a cinema. Late-night screenings of *Pepi, Luci, Bom and Other Girls on the Heap* drew crowds to Madrid's Alphaville multiplex at ungodly hours, and the management, out of a mixture of gratitude and good sense, provided a budget of twenty million pesetas (about $250,000).

That wasn't over-generous, and once again Almodóvar had to scratch around, especially since his screenplay, with its multiple strands and innumerable characters, called for a great number of sets and costumes. At the same time, shooting a film had by now ceased to be a risky adventure for him; the chief cameraman, Ángel Luis Fernández, was a professional and had worked with other directors connected with the Movida, such as Fernando Trueba.

As to his actors, Almodóvar picked names well known on the Madrid scene, starting with his buddy Fabio (Fanny) McNamara, and Cecilia Roth, whom he cast as a rock star, Sexilia. And this time he created two strong male roles; Imanol Arias, who later became a big star of Spanish cinema, plays Riza, a prince in exile who cruises the Madrid streets looking for pretty boys. He runs into Sadeq, a handsome terrorist and a member of an Islamist cell bent on assassinating Riza. Antonio Banderas, who plays him, was just twenty at the time.

Almodóvar couldn't have found a more expressive title for his film: a dozen characters in Madrid are sent down the most improbable pathways, motivated by every imaginable passion. Sexilia, a gynaecologist's daughter, is trying to overcome a childhood trauma, searching for fame on the stage and for power in bed, where she collects men; Riza is looking for instant satisfaction; Sadeq is a fanatic; Queti, the dry-cleaner, is a victim of her father's perverse, incestuous passion (she is under the influence of mind-altering drugs); Riza's mother, Toraya, the dethroned Empress, is trying to regain her covert ascendancy over the Emperor of Tiran. The film was made three years after the fall of the Shah, although Almodóvar assured Frederic Strauss, in *Conversations avec Pedro Almodóvar*, that he had written it before the Iranian revolution. But none of these passions are stable: Sexilia the nymphomaniac and Riza the man who loves men cannot break the law of irresistible and quasi-platonic attraction, and this 'labyrinth' suddenly turns into the straight and narrow path of a great love affair.

To the baroque complexity of this screenplay, Almodóvar added a realist story of the dying days of the Movida. As a director of photo-novels, he puts some quite repulsive images on the screen. Sexilia is the leader of a group of girls, Las Perras ('The Bitches'), who are the violent rivals of a group of boys. Through the fascination exerted by celebrities over ordinary people (Queti the dry-cleaner is a fan of Sexilia), the heady energy of the underground spreads to the rest of the city.

As it goes along, *Labyrinth of Passion* demonstrates that Almodóvar's ambitions as a scriptwriter were thwarted by his inexperience as a director. But even more strongly than in *Pepi, Luci, Bom and Other Girls on the Heap*, we recognize his ability to portray the true nature of human emotions and the desire for artifice and excess. When the film came out, after its presentation at the San Sebastián Festival in September 1982, he described it as follows in the Alphaville newsletter: 'On the one hand, there's an element of fairy tale, reminiscent of Ernst Marischka's *Sissi, imperatrice* (*Sissi the Empress*). A prince arrives in the city, and instead of falling in love with a princess, he falls for an ordinary girl, despite his high social status. The other part of the film is the "pop" story of two groups, one of girls, the other of boys, who hate each other but win the admiration of the city's fanatical music fans; and within that, there are several love stories. We could be talking about *Quadrophenia* — mods versus rockers — or *West Side Story*, Puerto Ricans versus the rest. Then there are the more obviously Spanish stories about lower-middle-class people and their world — their romantic magazines and recipes, their family and medical dramas.'

But in fact (though nobody could have guessed this in 1982), *Labyrinth of Passion* is also a kind of trailer for work to come: Toraya is the prototype for the bad mothers who appear regularly — those Antonio Banderas is lumbered with in *Law of Desire* and *Matador*, or Marisa Paredes's Becky del Páramo, who abandons her daughter in *High Heels* (1991); when she remembers a particular beach, Sexilia recovers a traumatic memory from her childhood. It's treated as comedy here, but this sequence will become a poignant moment in *High Heels*; the story of ordinary people that is sketched around Queti and her father will reappear in *What Have I Done to Deserve This?* and *Volver*; the encounter

Opposite page: Pedro Almodóvar and Fanny McNamara in *Labyrinth of Passion* (1982).

Below: Socorro Siva in *Labyrinth of Passion* (1982).

Fanny McNamara in
Labyrinth of Passion (1982).

of a man and a woman united in perversion (here nymphomania and sexual predation) will take a tragic turn in *Matador*.

Since they lacked the gift of foresight, the Madrid critics failed to detect these signs of things to come, and gave *Labyrinth* a cool reception, unlike audiences, who flocked to it. In 1982, the year in which Felipe González's Socialist Party came to power, Almodóvar branched out in several directions at once. He performed on stage and recorded disks with McNamara, made a pornographic photo-novel, *Toda tuya* (*All Yours*) and wrote a novel, *Fuego en las entrañas* (*Fire in the Guts*) illustrated by the Barcelona artist Mariscal.

A closed world of women

Almodóvar's name was not yet familiar outside Spain, but he was well known enough for Cristina S. Pascual, an actress looking for a leading role, to ask a favour from Luis Calvo, her producer husband: she wanted to make a film with 'Berlanga [the veteran director of *Bienvenue Mr. Marshall*], Zulueta [Ivan Zulueta had just made a daring feature film, *Arrebato* (*Ecstasy*)] and with Almodóvar'. Luis Calvo, a businessman who had gone into film production for the love of it, contacted the people involved. Almodóvar described this episode to Frédéric Strauss: 'I asked [Luis Calvo] if Cristina S. Pascual should play the lead in this project. He said, "Certainly not." But from the way he said it, I realized he meant, "Yes, of course."'

This hunch meant that Almodóvar got in ahead of Berlanga, who had also put in a bid. The problems associated with making a commissioned film were now added to the constraints suffered by a semi-professional with a restricted budget. In a somewhat perverse fashion, he wrote a terrific part for this actress, whose limits he must surely have suspected. As it was, he soon discovered them, and *Dark Habits*, a film technically more finished than its predecessors, suffers from a certain frustration at its centre.

Cristina S. Pascual plays Yolanda Bell, a bolero singer and heroin-user who takes refuge in a convent after her lover dies from an overdose. The community of the Humiliated Sisters of the Redemption is led by a Mother Superior who shares Yolanda's addiction, motivated by love. Her role, played by Julieta Serrano with grace and humour, is the film's emotional anchor. Almodóvar has created around her a little community whose 'names in religion' are ridiculous (Sister Manure, Sister Sewer Rat), played by Carmen Maura, Marisa Paredes, Lina Canaleja and Chus Lampreave. This is the first appearance in an Almodóvar film by this little woman with the big spectacles, here playing Sister Sewer Rat, the nun who writes porn novels. Almodóvar had been assiduously pursuing her since *Pepi, Luci, Bom and Other Girls on the Heap* and to this day she is the only actress to have worked continuously with a director who specializes in melodramatic casting without falling out with him in a spectacular way.

Having ceased to hope that Cristina S. Pascual would deliver what he had expected of her, he shifted the film's centre of gravity towards the nuns' community. They become the champions of the freedom to act creatively, and Julieta Serrano

From bolero to pogo music

A photograph of Pedro Almodóvar as a child shows him playing the mandolin; while a pupil of the Salesian Fathers he was a soloist with the choir. Like millions of teenagers of his generation, he found he could express through rock music feelings that were alien to the world of bolero (the sentimental Spanish version of this originally Caribbean form) and the *zarzuelas*, the operettas people listened to in La Mancha and Extremadura. In his first two films, rock music – or the Madrid punk version of it that was played with such passion and mockery during the Movida – helps to fuel the plot. But from *Labyrinth of Passion* onwards, another type of music makes a powerful entrance. Yolanda Bell, the 'fallen' heroine of *Dark Habits*, is not a rock star but a singer of boleros. Almodóvar's toing and froing between city and country has its musical equivalents, from 'Suck It To Me', written by Almodóvar and McNamara, which we hear in *Labyrinth of Passion*, to the most syrupy romantic numbers. In 1986, he stated on Spanish radio, 'I'm interested in all forms of music, and I don't reject any of them. None of them seems ancient or modern to me. I got my pop education in the sixties, but every melodramatic type of music has its place in my films – I'm talking about boleros, mambos, cumbia, salsa, and Latin American music in general. It's shameless music, in the best sense of the word. Nowadays the original soundtracks of Almodóvar's films contain very little rock music. Instead, they alternate between the quasi-classical elegance of his favourite composer, Alberto Iglesias, to archaeological layers of the most extreme sentimentality. The title of *Volver* is the same as that of a tango by Carlos Gardel, which is heard during the course of the film.

Opposite page: Cecilia Roth in *Dark Habits* (1983).

Right: Pedro Almodóvar playing the mandolin, with a classmate in the 1960s.

Following pages: Jaime Chávarri, Verónica Forque and Carmen Maura in *What Have I Done to Deserve This?* (1984).

plays the Mother Superior as a magnificent lover who combines, as the director himself has said, St John Bosco's thirst for redemption with Jean Genet's fascination with evil.

Once again, Almodóvar introduces his favourite themes and figures: inspired by a childhood memory, the scene in which Yolanda sings a bolero for the Mother Superior will appear in a different form in *Law of Desire* (1987) and *Bad Education*. *Dark Habits* also presents the first of his exclusively female closed worlds, a dominant theme in *Women on the Verge of a Nervous Breakdown* (1988) and *Volver*.

With the monastic associations of its title, *Dark Habits* is steeped in religion and it shows much greater understanding of the spiritual life than did those good folks who objected to its being selected – in a parallel section – at the Venice Film Festival. Lastly, this is the first time that Almodóvar drops the mask of comedy and burlesque and risks, venturing into melodrama. In a paradox not unheard of in the history of art, this commissioned work is the one that reveals its creator most clearly. 'There was a very private and personal reference there: I dared to talk about things I had never made public,' he admitted in the course of a TV broadcast in 1986.

The technical and artistic success of *Dark Habits* won him international recognition for the first time. The next step, which involved a return to comedy, turned him into one of the rising stars of European cinema, while in Spain his success with the public never waned.

All about mothers

It was Tesauro, Luis Calvo's company, that produced *What Have I Done to Deserve This?* Almodóvar thought for a long time before casting Carmen Maura in the leading role of Gloria, a mother at the end of her tether who takes amphetamines to help her get through her hours of work as a cleaner and feed her family. At the time, she was the star presenter of a TV programme. She was the incarnation of '*progre*' (permissive, trendy) Spain, and her image could not have been further from that of a cleaner on the brink of destitution. But she carries the film. This time, Almodóvar had found an actor who came up to scratch: the relationship between the film's centre and its periphery works perfectly. Gloria is the sun around whom her little world revolves: her teenage sons, her unfaithful husband, a taxi-driver and forger, her mother-in-law, obsessed with the idea of going back to the village (Chus Lampreave

Opposite page: Chus Lampreave in
What Have I Done to Deserve This?
(1984).

Above: the Spanish film poster of
What Have I Done to Deserve This?
(1984).

is seen here for the first time as the alter ego of
Francesca Caballero, Almodóvar's mother, who also,
incidentally, makes her first appearance in one of
her son's films), and her neighbours, Cristal the
prostitute (Verónica Forqué) and Juani the model
housewife (Kiti Manver).

When the film was released, Almodóvar, the
model son, described them all on Spanish radio: 'It's
a film in which different kinds of motherhood are
portrayed. Carmen Maura is the one who supports
the home, who carries all the burdens. There are
frustrated mothers, like Cristal, who would have
made a wonderful one, and there's a typical Spanish
mother, who terrifies me, the kind that gives you a
thrashing every five minutes, the tyrant-mothers
I see on the streets of Madrid, who slap their kids
when they fall over. And in among all these mothers, there's mine.'

At that time, Francesca Caballero was beginning to benefit from her elder son's celebrity. He had
become head of the family following the death of
his father, Antonio, shortly after the release of *Pepi,
Luci, Bom and Other Girls on the Heap*.

For the moment, he put aside the daring me-
lodramatics of *Dark Habits*, and *What Have I Done to
Deserve This?* , which marks a further extension of his
cinematographic repertory. The exterior sequences
were shot in the district of Concepción, the rest of
the film in the studio. Whereas in *Dark Habits* his
camera movements were relatively broad — he had
the luxury of using a real location, a convent due for
demolition — here he had to deal with the confined
spaces of a small flat, and to place the camera in
such a way that the static shots that make up most
of the film would work successfully. Almodovar
stands by the result, a kind of neo-realism, but a
'Spanish-style' neo-realism, full of black humour
and oblique satire (thanks to the censor), in the
tradition of the films of Luis García Berlanga from
the early 1960s or those made in Spain by Marco
Ferreri, of which the most memorable is *El cochecito*
(*The Little Car*, 1961).

But Almodóvar is unable to limit himself to
a single point of reference. At that time, he liked to
stress the vast distance separating his films from
those of Rainer Werner Fassbinder, but the character of Gloria is strongly reminiscent of some of
Fassbinder's female figures. He adds a frenetic,
American quality, and a strong whiff of TV soap

opera. And for the first time, he succeeds in imposing an overall discipline on this plethora of influences, characters and scraps of news footage. He's still provocative, but now this provocation is under firm directorial control, serving Almodóvar's central purpose: to portray his characters' poverty and deprivation through comedy, without taking away any of their dignity and complexity. Staggered by the wild inventiveness of the screenplay, audiences perhaps missed Almodóvar's increasing seriousness as a filmmaker.

What Have I Done to Deserve This? was shot in the early months of 1984, and was released in Spain in the autumn, taking over $7 million at the box office. It was presented at the New Directors, New Films festival in New York, and was the first of Almodóvar's films to be released commercially in the United States.

Early in 1985, he made a short feature for the public television channel *Trailer para los amantes del prohibido* (*Trailer for Lovers of the Forbidden*), a musical comedy loosely based on *Carmen*: a father leaves his wife and children for a 'creation' (the lovely Bibí Andersen, the transsexual who has appeared in Almodóvar's films up to and including *Kika*, 1993).

Blood and gold

Almodóvar describes his next film as his 'most abstract'. *Matador* turns on a series of oppositions: between the sexes, between the generations and between historical traditions. Of all his films, it is the one that comes closest to being a portrait of Spain. María Cardenal (Assumpta Serna) is a lawyer who defends political prisoners, Diego (Nacho Martínez) a retired bullfighter. The man and the woman both make a habit of killing their lovers.

Young Ángel (Antonio Banderas), who is taking lessons in bullfighting from Diego, attempts to rape his neighbour Eva, a model, played by Eva Cobo. Ángel's life is controlled by his mother (Julieta Serrano), a member of Opus Dei, while Eva is encouraged to look for fame and fortune by Pilar (Chus Lampreave), one of those mothers who, as her name (literally 'pillar') suggests, is the family's main support.

With a discipline that owes much to Alfred Hitchcock, Almodóvar casts a net in which all the characters are caught, including a sympathetic secret policeman (Eusebio Poncela), who has been dumped by a kindly psychotherapist (Carmen Maura).

Carmen Maura in *Law of Desire* (1987).

Opposite page: Assumpta Serna and Nacho Martínez in *Matador* (1986).

Despite the saturated colour of Ángel Luis Fernández's photography and Bernardo Bonezzi's extreme music, the film might create an impression almost of coldness, were it not for an astonishing performance by Antonio Banderas as a lost child, innocent even of the crime he has committed.

Matador was a big-budget film, and cost much more than those that preceded it. Almodóvar worked with the producer Andrés Vicente Gómez, who raised the then-impressive sum of almost $8 million, almost half of which came from official sources. When the Socialist government was elected, the filmmaker Pilar Miró (who had just adapted the novel *El Crimen de Cuenca*, by Nobel prize-winner Camilo José Cela) was appointed Head of Cinema at the Ministry of Culture. She set up a system of direct funding for film production, from which *Matador* benefited. Agustín Almodóvar, who had given up his intended career in chemical engineering, and was working with his brother on a day-to-day basis, realized how easy it had been for the producer of *Matador* to raise the finance for the film. When Andrés Vicente Gómez, in the brothers' opinion, did

the bare minimum to promote the film in Spain and abroad, Francesca Caballero's younger son was in no doubt as to the path they should take: from now on, they would be their own producers. 'I had made five films before that, and it was like having five children with five different fathers,' explained Almodóvar to *Manhattan* magazine. 'You think of them as your own, but parental authority rests with the father and you have no say in their destiny.' Their company, founded in early 1986, would be called El Deseo ('Desire'), and the first film made under that name, *Law of Desire*.

The man who was a woman

What better way could there be to launch this new independent venture than to score a hit with a film that was both a new departure and a summation of all the experience accumulated so far? 'It was as if I were starting out again, as if I were making my first film and that for the first time it involved a character who was very close to me, working in the same profession, and that's typical of a first film, even if I waited for my sixth one before

Men, an instruction manual

From the average girls of 1980 to the village women of 2006, the director of *Pepi, Luci, Bom and Other Girls on the Heap* and *Volver* has had time to establish his reputation as a director of women. But when *What Have I Done to Deserve This?* came out, he declared: 'In my next film, the main character will be a man. I'm through with giving parts only to women.'

Matador offered his first big role to Antonio Banderas, who plays a disturbed teenager. Banderas is the only actor who can pride himself on having worked consistently with Almodóvar, remaining with him through the six years from *Labyrinth of Passion* to *Tie Me Up! Tie Me Down!* Clearly, Almodóvar found in the young Andalucian actor someone who

was malleable enough for him not to experience his usual frustration in dealing with actors in general, and men in particular. Whether playing a victim (*Matador*), a criminal (*Law of Desire*) or a seducer (*Tie Me Up! Tie Me Down!*), Antonio Banderas has managed to vary his roles, while most of the other actors Almodóvar has employed have worked with him only once. Almodóvar is always attracted to the most popular actors of the moment, but it would seem that the results rarely meet his expectations. He fired Jorge Sanz shortly after they began shooting *Live Flesh* (1997), and has attributed the lack of empathy that the character of Ángel elicits in *Bad Education* to reserve on the part of Gael García Bernal.

Similarly, the artistic failure of *Kika* was largely due to the mediocre performance he obtained from Peter Coyote.

Nevertheless, Almodóvar's 'masculine' films generally mark an advance in his development. With the exception of *Tie Me Up! Tie Me Down!*, which is an exceptionally simple heterosexual love story, in Almodóvar's eyes all these feature films present male couples: the film director Pablo Quintero and the rent-boy Antonio in *Law of Desire*, David, the paraplegic police officer and Victor the orphan in *Live Flesh*. This duality is a source of tragedy, with one exception: Benigno and Marco in *Talk to Her*. This time Almodóvar introduced new faces: Javier Cámara was known only to Spanish television

audiences, and Dario Grandinetti had played minor roles in his native Argentina. For once, the men occupy all the space (both the women are in a coma), not tearing each other apart but offering mutual comfort. This time of peace did not last long, as it was followed by the unrelieved blackness of the perverse passions in *Bad Education*.

One could say that after each film that gives men a better deal, Almodóvar feels the need to create another society ruled by women: after *Law of Desire* came *Women on the Verge of a Nervous Breakdown*, after *Live Flesh*, *All About My Mother*, and after *Bad Education*, *Volver*.

Above: Gael García Bernal (left) in *Bad Education* (2004) and Antonio Banderas (right) in *Law of Desire* (1987).

Following pages: Carmen Maura and Pablo Eusebio Poncela in *Law of Desire* (1987).

doing it. But that's a false impression; there's no autobiography in *Law of Desire*, it's a piece of fiction', said Almodóvar to *Interviú* magazine when the film was released early in 1987.

His apparent alter ego is called Pablo Quintero, and he has the smooth face and open expression of Eusebio Poncela, the physical antithesis of the real-life Pedro. The opening sequences of *Law of Desire* are cruel and highly comic. We see a naked young man on a bed, masturbating to the instructions given by a man off-screen. But they are not a director's instructions to an actor, since at the crucial moment we discover that the voices of the rent-boy and his client are those of two anonymous men who are voicing-over the actors in an auditorium. This twist was not devised by Almodóvar but by Pablo Quintero, since what we've just seen is the final sequence of the protagonist's latest film, *El Paradigma del mejillón* (The Paradigm of the Mussel), of which we've been given a preview. Quintero's vanity and loneliness are presented with a coldness that verges on the relentless, and for a moment we wonder if there isn't an element of mortification on the part of a director whose fame was increasing by the day. Describing this fictional character in his interviews with Nuria Vidal, Almodóvar agrees that the character he has created represents himself: 'a person who has followed his own path in a very clear, determined fashion since [he was] very young, [which] amounts to what people call egoism or egocentrism.'

But the film only really gets going with the entrance of Antonio Benítez (Antonio Banderas), a young man who offers to replace the young lover whom Pablo Quintero has allowed to go on vacation. Benítez has problems in accepting his sexual orientation and a tendency to be jealous that give his passion a tragic, criminal dimension. The only help Pablo can count on is that of his brother, who has now become his sister, Tina, the transsexual who is bringing up Ada, a model's daughter. Ada finds a perfect father figure in Pablo. Tina is an actress, and she is studying her part in Jean Cocteau's *La Voix humaine* in a production by her brother.

Antonio's destructive passion for Pablo would have been enough material in itself for a melodrama, but the counterpoint of Tina's quest (her name is the feminine equivalent of the diminutive 'Tinín', Agustín Almodóvar's nickname) highlights the gulf that separates artists from the rest of humanity, the terrible parasitic power that fiction exerts over real life. Almodóvar has frequently said that for him, fiction makes life better. This time he shows its costs and dangers, as he will do again in a melancholy vein in *The Flower of My Secret*, and in a black one in *Bad Education*.

On this occasion, the tone is both sombre and flamboyant, and the comedy serves only to counterbalance it. Almodóvar shows increasing control over his plot and its multiplicity of characters; the formal experiments of *Matador* have been assimilated and give the film a discreet stylishness that periodically bursts out in moments of breathtaking sensuality: the fire hydrant that drenches Carmen Maura in a Madrid street at night is every bit as stunning as the air vent that once lifted up Marilyn Monroe's skirt.

Law of Desire is Almodóvar's first major film and is a distillation of a lifetime's perceptions, learning experiences, and emotional and aesthetic feelings. He has retained everything, from the starvation of the senses he describes when talking about his childhood in La Mancha, to the bombardment of sounds and images that was the Movida. And while in his early days he often used collage, as much out of an affinity with that pre-eminently post-modern form than out of necessity, in *Law of Desire* he created a totally fluid, coherent work. It contains the oppositions that are at the heart of his films — desire and isolation, burlesque and melodrama, night-time in the city and the light in the fields, this time organized around the vision of a man who sees just as clearly what is within as what is around him.

Law of Desire was presented in competition at the 1987 Berlin Film Festival on 7 February, the day on which it was released in Spain. At a party in Berlin, Almodóvar was again able to take advantage of the fact that she was little-known in the film world to pass Carmen Maura off as a star of Spanish porn films. *Law of Desire* took the Teddy Award, a 'gay' prize that did not greatly please Almodóvar, who was at pains to point out, 'This not a film about homosexuals, it's not a militant film … The problem it poses is that of a life at the mercy of a passion.' It was to take another film for Almodóvar to be recognized throughout the world and fêted in Hollywood and Paris.

A Director at the Foot of Mount Olympus

From *Women on the Verge of a Nervous Breakdown* to *The Flower of My Secret*

Pedro Almodóvar and the cast of *High Heels* (1991): Marisa Paredes, Victoria Abril, Miguel Bosé, Bibi Andersen and Miriam Díaz-Aroca.

Nervous breakdown in Hollywood

Almodóvar didn't waste any time. He resumed his habitual winter shooting schedule, which he had disrupted to make *Law of Desire*. By November, he was in a studio in Madrid, making a feature film, already entitled *Women on the Verge of a Nervous Breakdown*. Interviewed by a journalist from *El País*, he said he was aiming for 'the look of a 1950s American comedy'. To sceptics who couldn't see the director of *Law of Desire* reviving the innocent delights of Doris Day and Rock Hudson, he said, 'The characters don't take drugs, don't drink, they don't even smoke because the doctor advises against it. They don't even have time to get up to anything dirty. I've got an immaculate comedy on my hands.'

To hear him speak, you would never guess the film was first conceived of as an adaptation of *La Voix humaine*. But since Cocteau's text — a monologue by a woman abandoned by her lover — doesn't last long enough for a full-length feature, Almodóvar started to imagine the forty-eight hours before her lover left her. It was once things got under way that *Women on the Verge of a Nervous Breakdown* became a pure comedy that turns the tragic figures of Almodóvar's preceding films inside out, making them objects of scorn and amusement. Around Pepa (Carmen

Maura), who would like to leave her flat after she herself has been abandoned by Ivan, her lover, there forms a group of women all of whom are on the brink of an explosive crisis: there's Candela (María Barranco), fleeing the police, who are in pursuit of her Islamist terrorist lover (Almodóvar admits he borrowed this situation from the life of a woman friend who had been involved with an ETA militant); Lucía (Julieta Serrano), who preceded Pepa in Ivan's bed; and Marisa (Rossy de Palma, whose stunning profile the world would discover here after glimpsing it in *Law of Desire*), the partner of Carlos, the son that Ivan and Lucía had together. All of them embark, with greater or lesser success, on a steep learning curve in living without men.

In directing this hectic screenplay, Almodóvar pulled out all the stops to ensure that it had maximum appeal for a mass audience. He had the set of the flat built in the studio, and exploits both the kitschy and glamorous aspects of its fake roofterrace, looking out over a filmed Madrid. The success the film was to enjoy was probably not unconnected with the fact that, for the first time, the financial resources at the director's disposal exactly matched his ambition. Ángel Luis Fernández was now replaced by José Luis Alcaine. Almodóvar told

Julieta Serrano in *Women on the Verge of a Nervous Breakdown* (1988).

'A banquet for the senses', by Manuel Vázquez Montalbán

In the early 1980s, I had a flash of feminine intuition and prophesied that the Transition [to democracy] had found in [José] Barrionuevo [the Socialist deputy mayor of Madrid and Minister of the Interior] its hairdresser and in Almodóvar its poet. That's how my *Crónica Sentimental de la Transición* [*Sentimental Chronicle of the Transition*, 1985] ends, shortly after a famous police raid on a neighbourhood of Madrid and my transformation into an Almodóvar addict. The pedantic graphologists of cinema accuse Almodóvar of linguistic eclecticism, perhaps without understanding that, in years to come, Almodóvar will be seen as the missing link between cinema as a rigorously modern art and the cinema that will emerge after post-modernism's plague of langoustines. Like the writers in their twenties who

start out by digesting films, comics and the work of Boris Vian ... a handful of new, international filmmakers have taken the cultural inheritance of cinema and cannibalized it. They have assimilated it and drawn from it a personal vision of cinema, based exclusively on cinema. That would not be enough to define the uniqueness of Almodóvar's signature, if we did not take into account the uniqueness of his perspective.

That Almodóvar is from La Mancha, that he is polysexual, innocent, and a survivor who is both tough and tender, all help to explain the remaining fifty percent of his ability to astonish us. All the elements that form him clearly come from the same cinematic family tree, with whose Hispano-Celtic roots he maintains a relationship that is both loving and mocking.

One needs to have an eye that is consciously that of an outsider to come up with the twentieth century's best playlet (*What Have I Done to Deserve This?*), a flat, post-surrealist tragedy (*Matador*), the best Fassbinder film, improved by the irony that Fassbinder has never been able to muster (*Law of Desire*) and a magisterial defence of the war between the sexes that in Spain always, always, requires the love potion of a gaspacho updated by being made in a blender (*Women on the Verge of a Nervous Breakdown*).

Almodóvar's ambiguous eye becomes the audience's ambiguous eye, forced to question established values, not by way of a private orgy, as with Buñuel, but in a banquet for the senses. I now await *Tie Me Up! Tie Me Down!* with the little bit of blind faith I still possess. I know I'm

going to see something surprising that will redefine what I either know already or have simply seen thousands of times. There truly is an Almodóvar touch, and it explains the uniqueness of a filmography already sufficiently solid and varied that it cannot be reduced to the product of an off-the-shelf Movida.

Etymologically speaking, the word 'insolent' [in the sense of 'cheeky'] comes from the Latin *insolens*, which can mean unusual or excessive. Almodóvar is harmoniously excessive, over the top but precise, guided by the inherited syntax of the entire history of cinema. In other words, the entire history of a language.

This is an extract from an article published in *El País*, 23 January 1990. Manuel Vázquez Montalbán (1939–2003) was a novelist and journalist.

Left: María Barranco, Rossy de Palma and Antonio Banderas in *Women on the Verge of a Nervous Breakdown* (1988).

Opposite page: Rossy de Palma, Pedro Almodóvar, Carmen Maura, Agustín Almodóvar and Kiti Manver in front of the Italian poster of *Women on the Verge of a Nervous Breakdown* (1988).

Following pages: Carmen Maura in *Women on the Verge of a Nervous Breakdown* (1988).

Frédéric Strauss that his former director of photography was 'less on the ball' during the shooting of *Law of Desire*. With a director who demands of his technicians that they 'prove themselves as if every film were their first', it is inevitable that there will be partings of the ways. Bernardo Bonezzi composed the music for *Women on the Verge of a Nervous Breakdown*, but it was the last time he would collaborate with Almodóvar.

From that point onwards, a sort of global misunderstanding arose: Almodóvar was the brilliant clown of a Spain on the road to modernization, as if the Movida had not been over long ago, and as if he did not already have behind him a diverse body of work that included burlesque and tragedy, melodrama and film noir. In fact, the formal luxuriance of *Women on the Verge of a Nervous Breakdown* creates a very incomplete idea of Almodóvar's style, which pays attention only to the sets (preferably built in the studio) and costumes; borrowings from collections illustrated in popular magazines have given way to more sophisticated acts of piracy, and Julieta Serrano wears Courrèges outfits adapted by the costume designer.

For the moment, there was no reason to deny the fabulous success of *Women on the Verge of a Nervous Breakdown*, especially in Spain, where by the end of its run it had been seen by three million people, still the best performance by any of Almodóvar's films. The director who had such a stormy relationship with his country's film industry became its darling overnight. The ceremony of the Goyas, Madrid's equivalent of the Oscars, was a triumph. The film was nominated in every category and came away with five awards.

The film opened in Madrid in February 1988 and broke records all over the world. It marked Almodóvar's first success in France, attracting audiences of over 600,000. In the United States, where it was distributed by Orion Classics, *Women on the Verge of a Nervous Breakdown* was a box-office phenomenon, taking over $7 million, ten times its production costs. Most important of all, it was nominated for an Oscar for best foreign film. Early in 1989, Almodóvar went to Los Angeles to promote it. There he met Billy Wilder, who warned him against being seduced by the siren song of Hollywood.

On 29 March, Pedro Almodóvar saw the Oscar go to Bille August, for *Pelle the Conqueror*, and he made public his break with Carmen Maura, for reasons that remain mysterious, but which no doubt include the effects of friction over time. At the last moment, he took her name off his list of personal invitations to the ceremony, and she had to go alone. This episode created a climate of mistrust towards him on the part of Spanish audiences. It filled pages in the Madrid newpapers, which emphasized his roughness and Maura's popularity. She has kept a discreet silence on the subject, while Almodóvar justifies himself with some degree of tact: 'I have problems with Carmen that go back a long way. I hoped they would resolve themselves, but they didn't,' he told *El País*. For years, Carmen Maura has been presented as Almodóvar's 'muse', but she describes herself as a 'self-service' actress, from whom directors take what they want, what they're looking for. It would be seventeen years before the two worked together again, on *Volver*.

The ties that bind

It wasn't long before Almodóvar introduced Carmen Maura's successor, in the person of Victoria Abril. She was already a star in France and Spain. She had appeared in Jean-Jacques Beineix's *La Lune dans le caniveau* (*The Moon in the Gutter*, 1983), which was presented at Cannes, and in Manuel Gutiérrez Aragón's *La Noche mas hermosa* (*The Most Beautiful Night*, 1985), a sentimental comedy that was very successful in Spain. She would be star and victim in *Tie Me Up! Tie Me Down!*, a film of which Almodóvar said, on the first day's shooting (4 July 1989), that it would portray the efforts of the leading character Ricki (played by Antonio Banderas) to 'find a place in consumer society and somone with whom to share it'. Its other themes would be 'brotherhood, drug addiction, the creative process and [his] preoccupation with cinema and his own survival'.

All this is embodied in the screenplay: newly discharged from the psychiatric hospital where he has spent a number of years, Ricki goes in search of

Carmen Maura remembers

When I met Almodóvar, he was very young, but already unique. He was like no one else, he took my breath away. I was acting in Sartre's *Les Mains Sales*, in which he had a small part. It was my first big play. I had previously done some cabaret, a few walk-on parts on TV, and some stupid comedies that went on seedy little tours. I was happy, because I was making a living. At home they'd all said, 'You won't last three months.' That's what they hoped, and they didn't give me any money. I was no longer married ... To the rest of the cast, I was a middle-class women with a hobby, and to my parents, a whore ...

But in fact, I knew a lot, especially how to adapt, and that's what Almodóvar liked. We're different, but we have the same sense of humour. We started filming together right away. Without a penny, of course, and surreptitiously, in the street, speaking our lines into lapel-mikes because we didn't have a permit. We only worked at weekends and it took us two years to finish the first film. In the meantime, we worked for a living and looked for money to make the film. Almodóvar's humour seems very aggressive to us Spaniards. He talks about everything that's strictly forbidden – homosexuality and drugs – and he attacks religious education ...

Pedro's secret is his mother. She's a real working-class woman, with a keen, direct intelligence. She still lives in her home village and has never wished to see her son's films. But she loves the prizes they win. Pedro brings them to her, and she puts them on the wall, or on her mantelpiece ... And she plays small parts. She's thrilled because she earns what she considers a lot of money for just a day's work, and because she can keep the clothes she wears in the film. Pedro is sophisticated, but he has inherited from his mother his particular form of intelligence. And he likes that about me, too. In Venice, he said I brought him down to earth. I was happy. I always try to lead him in the direction of a practical life without taking him out of his own world.

At the moment, Almodóvar is well established in Spain, and my parents would like me to continue working with him. But I think I need a rest from him ... Pedro has a different career from me, and different ambitions. He'll work with big stars. He'll see what that means. He phones you and asks you to be at such and such a place within an hour, and you're there. He won't be able to do that with Jessica Lange or Meryl Streep. I still love him, and I'll be the first to go and see his new film. We've worked, travelled and had a laugh together. For a whole year we were hardly ever apart ... It's harder to deal with success than to live with difficulties. When life's difficult, you tap yourself on the shoulder and buck yourself up. When you're successful, everyone introduces you as if you were a different person. In fact, you haven't changed at all. I need to get myself back again.

This is an extract from an interview published in *Le Monde*, 2 February 1989.

Opposite page: Pedro Almodóvar directing Victoria Abril and Antonio Banderas on the set of *Tie Me Up! Tie Me Down!* (1990).

Right: Pedro Almodóvar with Carmen Maura on the set of *Dark Habits* (1983).

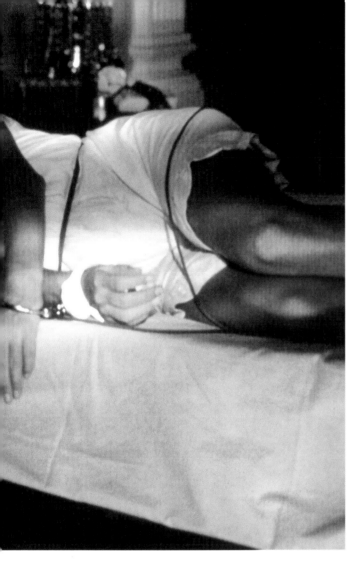

Above: Antonio Banderas and
Victoria Abril in *Tie Me Up!
Tie Me Down!* (1990).

Opposite page: Pedro Almodóvar
and Victoria Abril on the set of *Tie
Me Up! Tie Me Down!* (1990).

Marina (Victoria Abril), a woman he had met once,
during one of his rare moments of freedom. Marina
is an actress trying to give up making porn films and
move into 'legitimate' cinema, under the influence
of a hemiplegic director (the veteran actor Francisco
Rabal, who had appeared in films by Luis Buñuel,
notably *Nazarin*, in 1958). The young man kidnaps
his actress and keeps her prisoner, until they form
an improbably idyllic relationship, which ends in
an escape to the young man's home village.

In his *Conversations avec Pedro Almodóvar*, Frédéric
Strauss managed for once to persuade Almodóvar
to retrace the origins of this story: while he was
filming *Women on the Verge of a Nervous Breakdown*
the idea came to him to use the film set, as such.
In other words, to imagine that a group of escaped
prisoners take refuge on a deserted film set — the
situation is slightly reminiscent of William Wyler's
The Desperate Hours. But the apparently abandoned
set still has to be used for the end-of-filming party.
That's when one of the fugitives falls in love with
one of the actresses, whom he eventually impris-
ons in the studio toilets.

Almodóvar wasn't able to shoot a second
film on the set of *Women on the Verge of a Nervous
Breakdown*, as he had hoped, and when shooting
had finished he went back to his other idea, whose
theme gradually shifted until it became the pos-
sibility of love under constraint. The final result
shows the traces of that process; American femi-
nists accused the film of defending violence against
women, but its theatrical quality, created by both
the victim's profession and the artifice of a film-set,
makes a literal interpretation impossible. *Tie Me Up!
Tie Me Down!* is truly a film about love, in which the
protagonists, who are young and beautiful, win the
audience's sympathy despite the bizarre nature of
their mutual attraction.

Although the public and the critics awaited
Tie Me Up! Tie Me Down! with a certain amount of
spitefulness, it was a success. Not as successful as
Women on the Verge of a Nervous Breakdown, but it con-
firmed Almodóvar's standing as a director with an
international reputation. But in the United States,
one particular sequence upset the censors at the
Motion Picture Association of America, the orga-
nization responsible for classifying films. In it we
see Victoria Abril taking a bath in the company of
a little plastic diver that you have to wind up to

make him swim under water. The little man dives between the actress's open thighs in a movement that prefigures that of the minuscule lover, the star of the silent film Almodóvar would insert into *Talk to Her* (2002), twelve years later.

That was enough for *Tie Me Up! Tie Me Down!* to be threatened with an 'X' classification. In April 1990, Almodóvar picked up his pen to attack the hypocrisy of the American censors. Shortly afterwards, its new American distributor, the Weinstein brothers' company, Miramax, started an action to get this ignominious classification altered, but with no success. Miramax was forced to release the film without classification, which meant it was automatically barred from some cinemas and lost most of its media advertising. Despite all that, *Tie Me Up! Tie Me Down!* took over $4 million at the box office.

The abandoned child

In early 1991, Anagrama published a collection of texts that Almodóvar had written during the previous ten years. The *pièce de résistance* was a novel, *Patty Diphusa*. To mark its publication, Almodóvar looked back at his wild years, telling *El País* that it was 'a faithful portrait' of what he had been like during the Movida, but that he 'preferred to live the way he lived now, because although the pace was much more fun, it was impossible to keep it going, and the sex and drugs would have got the better of [him].'

At the time, he was preparing to start shooting *High Heels*, the first fruit of a strange association that would last until 1994 and would bring together El Deseo and Ciby 2000, the production company founded by Francis Bouygues, the French construction and media magnate. Bouygues, who

Above: Victoria Abril with Miguel Bosé (left) and Marisa Paredes (right) in *High Heels* (1991).

Opposite page: Victoria Abril in *Tie Me Up! Tie Me Down!* (1990).

Following pages: Victoria Abril and Marisa Paredes in *High Heels* (1991).

had acquired in 1987 the TV channel TF1, promising to promote cultural programmes in a big way, made good in cinema the promise he had failed to keep in television, and he financed the films of David Lynch, Abbas Kiarostami and Jane Campion.

Before he shot the first scene of his next film, Almodóvar had to deal with the sudden defection of his star. Antonio Banderas was supposed to play the leading role in *High Heels*, but at the last moment, he decided to accept an offer from Hollywood, a substantial subsidiary role in *The Mambo Kings* (Arne Glimcher, 1992), an adaptation of a popular novel. This time, the break did not cause a scandal, but shooting was delayed until April, while a replacement was found. He was Miguel Bosé, a singer, the son of the actress Lucía Bosé and the bullfighter Luis Miguel Dominguín. Victoria Abril plays Rebeca, a TV newscaster who lives on the memory of her mother, the singer Becky del Páramo, who abandoned Rebeca to pursue her career in Mexico. To comfort herself, Rebeca has married Manuel (Feodor Atkine), an old lover of her mother's, and hangs out

at a cabaret where Letal (Miguel Bosé), a transvestite, impersonates Becky.

The bad mother who abandons her child is at the centre of the film. Almodóvar gave the part to Marisa Paredes, with whom he had not worked since *Dark Habits*. The actress has to express both the artist's tremendous egoism and the unnatural mother's growing repentance. When Manuel is murdered, there appears on the scene a judge who resembles Letal, but with a beard. In this world, the law is elusive, ill-defined – once again, nothing counts but the feelings that bring people together and drive them apart. After Rebeca is accused of Manuel's murder, a terrific sequence shows her alone in prison, listening on the radio to snatches of the concert her mother is giving to celebrate her return to Madrid. The distress of the abandoned child behind bars is matched by the helplessness of the star weeping on the stage. In the interviews he gave when it was released, Almodóvar constantly mentioned the influence of Douglas Sirk's melodramas, pointing out that Marisa Paredes has her hair

styled like Lana Turner in *Imitation of Life* (1959). In addition, the screenplay alludes to the real life of the scandal-ridden American star, whose daughter murdered Tirner's lover. The melodrama is further accentuated by Becky del Páramo's repertoire: the lament 'Piensa in mi', sung by Luz Casals, was a hit all over Europe.

The premiere of *High Heels*, on 22 October 1991, was the occasion for a spectacular party to which guests were transported in giant high-heeled shoes, gliding through the Madrid night. Almodóvar was the city's hero. The previous year, he had been Madonna's host on the Spanish leg of her world tour, even announcing he was shooting a short film with her. In 1993, he played a more than active part in the return to the stage of Chavela Vargas. Then in her seventies, the Costa Rican singer who had been Frida Kahlo's lover came out of retirement at the invitation of Almodóvar, who used her songs in *Kika*, *The Flower of My Secret* and *Live Flesh*.

The secret of serenity

Nevertheless, the Spanish critics gave *High Heels* a lukewarm reception. Two years later, they were positively hostile to *Kika*, the least likable of Almodóvar's films. Again co-financed by Ciby 2000, and again starring Victoria Abril, the film has a strange brutality. Just as Mary Shelley's monster is not actually called Frankenstein, Kika is not the name of the character played by Victoria Abril, a newscaster and the producer of a reality TV show in which she goes in search of life's victims. Kika (Verónica Forqué) is a make-up artist, full of bounce and drive, who lives with Ramón, a photographer whom she met when she was asked to make him look presentable for his funeral. But Ramón wasn't quite dead and Kika brought him back to life — him and the heavy baggage of his past: his mother's suicide and the mysterious part played in it by his stepfather, Nicholas (Peter Coyote). Kika resumes an old liaison with Nicholas when he returns to Madrid. But she is harassed by the hatred of Andrea Caracortada ('Scarface') (Victoria Abril), who, by a perverse coincidence, took the opportunity of filming Kika's rape by an actor in pornographic films, recently escaped from prison.

In a 'statement of intent' that he published in *El País*, as he had already done for his previous film (and what better way of getting out of giving an interview?), Almodóvar said, 'I decided to make Kika unfailingly optimistic, but the three other characters wrote themselves.' And in fact *Kika* is the director's only film in which the characters are seen as all black or all white, as he has admitted himself. He paints the soul of Andrea Caracortada in unrelieved black, without an ounce of compassion, and

Above: Pedro Almodóvar directing Agustín Almodóvar (left) and Francesca Caballero (right) on the set of *Kika* (1993).

Below: Victoria Abril in *Kika* (1993).

Opposite page: Pedro Almodóvar on the set of *Kika* (1993).

Following pages: Verónica Forqué, Santiago Lajusticia and Rossy de Palma in *Kika* (1993).

Pages 58–9: Marisa Paredes and Imanol Arias in *The Flower of My Secret* (1995).

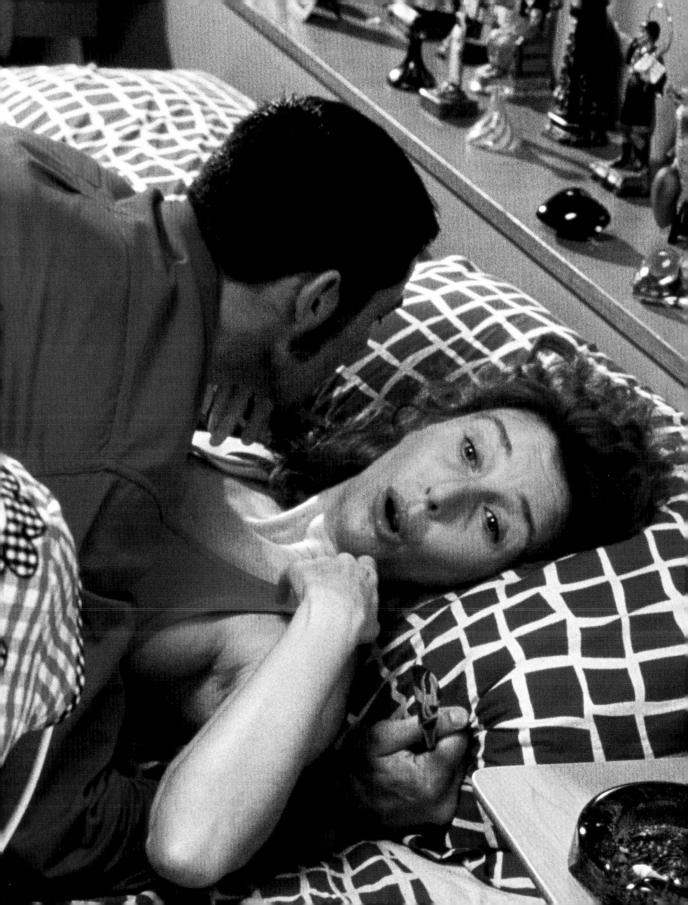

Peter Coyote's Nicholas (the American actor often seems as though he regretted applying for a Spanish visa) is a petty crook of no particular interest.

The story contains a violent anger against TV shows, and the financial backers of TF1, who at the time were wondering what to do with Ciby 2000 after the death of its founder in 1992, must surely have been amused. This brutality makes *Kika* often funny and provocative, but it adds up to a film that is rarely moving and sometimes unpleasant. Until then, it could have been said that Almodóvar was making elegant variations on a theme, but it now looked as if he was churning out the same old thing. The public was put off by this aggressiveness, and the film received a poor response in Spain and the United States. It only did well in France, where it attracted an audience of over 600,000.

As if by chance, the next story to emerge from Pedro Almodóvar's imagination — *The Flower of My Secret* — was that of someone who is a prisoner of the world she has created and now detests. Leo Macias (Marisa Paredes) writes romantic novels under the pseudonym Amanda Gris. But as Almodóvar said to *El País* in February 1995, during filming, 'She sees everything in black.' Her marriage to Paco (Imanol Arias, who is very stylish in a particularly unrewarding role), a senior officer attached to Nato, is on the rocks, and Leo is sickened by the inanities that flow from Amanda's pen. She tries to change direction by writing a violent thriller and by trying out as a book reviewer with *El País*. But the first book they give her is the latest title by Amanda Gris.

Leo is in the depths of despair, which needs no violence to express itself. Speaking of the shoot, Marisa Paredes commented, in a piece published in *Cahiers du cinéma*, that the atmosphere was gentler, calmer, than it had been on the set of *High Heels*. In fact, *The Flower of My Secret* is a film about appeasement and reconciliation with oneself. In it Almodóvar explores themes not previously seen in his work. The first sequence shows a group of doctors trying to persuade a mother to donate her dying son's organs. It ends with a twist (like the masturbation scene that opens *Law of Desire*), since it is only

Left: Marisa Paredes in
The Flower of My Secret (1995).

Right: Pedro Almodóvar with
Marisa Paredes on the set of *The
Flower of My Secret* (1995).

a simulation exercise organized by Betty, Leo's best friend, designed to train doctors. Here Almodóvar approaches the frontiers of life and death, which he will explore more deeply in *All About My Mother*, *Talk to Her* and *Volver*.

But most importantly, faced with the break-up of her marriage and the block in her professional life, Leo turns to her family. Almodóvar had not used Chus Lampreave since *Women on the Verge of a Nervous Breakdown*. Here she plays Leo's mother, an old, almost blind, woman, exiled in Madrid with her other daughter and dreaming of return-ing to her village.

When her dream finally comes true, she returns with her eldest daughter, to whom she recites a simple bucolic poem, which was actually written by Francesca Caballero. The sequences that show the writer in the country, slipping into the peaceful rhythm of village life, have a humour that is totally devoid of irony. The simplicity and sweet-ness of *The Flower of My Secret* are underlined by the parallel story of Ángel, Blanca, Leo's cleaning lady.

Played by Joaquín Cortés and Manuela Vargas — both professional dancers — these characters, poor people who have to take tortuous routes to practise their art, remind us that the freedom to create is a luxury beyond the reach of many artists.

With *The Flower of My Secret*, Almodóvar made up his differences with Spanish audiences and critics, and above all with himself. The film drew an audience of almost one million and was an international triumph, although the jury who awarded the Goyas haughtily ignored it. Lastly, it marked Almodóvar's first collaboration with the composer Alberto Iglesias and the Brazilian director of photography Affonso Beato, who had worked with the American underground direc-tor, Jim McBride, as well as with Agnès Varda and Jean-Daniel Pollet. Each in his own way, Beato and Iglesias helped create what would be Almodóvar's new style, that of an artist with total mastery of his vision, no longer needing to resort to provo-cation or excess, yet without surrendering to the dictates of reason and good taste.

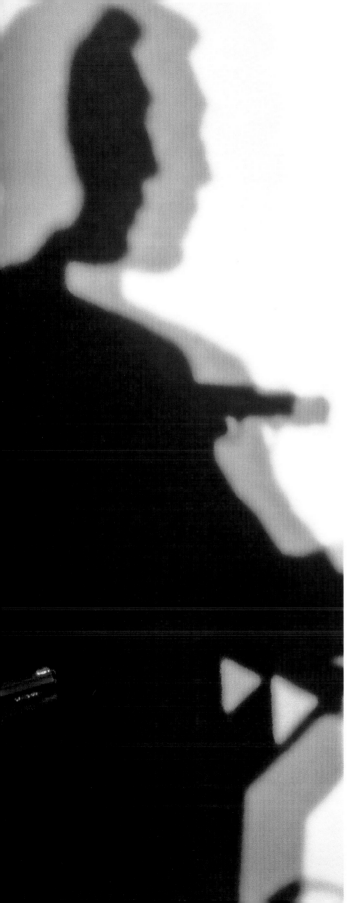

Master Works
From *Live Flesh*
to *Broken Embraces*

Javier Bardem and José Sancho in
Live Flesh (1997).

Black is black

This new mastery was demonstrated first of all in a new venture for Almodóvar: the genre film. For the first time, he adapted a text that he hadn't written himself, a crime novel by Ruth Rendell, entitled *Live Flesh*. Another innovation was that he wrote the screenplay for *Live Flesh* in collaboration with a young Spanish novelist, Ray Lorriga. Lastly, the cast includes none of the actors with whom he had worked regularly in the past; he preferred to introduce some new faces from Spanish cinema, and a little-known Italian actress.

Filming started badly. After a few days, the actor Jorge Sanz, a young up-and-coming lead in Spain, was let go, though his considerable reputation remained intact. He was replaced by Liberto Rabal, Francisco Rabal's grandson. The film presented entirely new difficulties for Almodóvar: it begins with an historical reconstruction of Madrid as it was in 1969, and continues with an action sequence.

The prologue shows Victor's birth on a bus, on the night when the Franco regime proclaimed a state of emergency, following separatist agitation in the Basque region. On the soundtrack we hear the voice of the Minister of the Interior, Manuel Fraga Irribarne, the future founder of the

Partido Popular, José María Aznar's party. The circumstances in which he comes into the world mean that the child and his mother, a young prostitute called Isabel (Penélope Cruz, working with Almodóvar for the first time), will enjoy a lifetime's free travel on the Madrid bus network. In the action sequence, which takes place twenty years later, Victor, who is now a pizza delivery boy gets into the house of Helena (Francesca Neri), a drug addict with whom he lost his virginity, and has a violent argument with her. Called by the neighbours, two police officers, David (Javier Bardem) and Sancho (José Sancho), break down the door. In a fight, David is injured (he will be paralysed for life) and Victor is arrested.

Following this two-part introduction, *Live Flesh* shifts again in time. Victor has spent four years in prison. When he comes out, this young man, an updated version of Antonio in *Tie Me Up! Tie Me Down!*, tries after his own fashion to restore the ties among the characters of the drama: David, who now uses a wheelchair, is living with Helena; Sancho is still a policeman and is haunted by the thought that his wife Clara (Ángela Molina) is deceiving him. Before he gets even with Helena, who humiliated him, Victor seduces Clara so that she can initiate him in the art of love.

Like his hero, Almodóvar redefines the relationships between characters. In a traditional thriller, the crime determines the relationships, with their underlying desires and emotions. In this case, the screenplay has some of the characteristics of the genre — puzzles to be solved, responsibilities to be determined — but it alters its weave, and is ultimately interested only in the desires of the five main characters. Almodóvar has got over the vengeful impulses that marred *Kika*. The issue in this film is not to determine, through a police investigation or a trial, the guilt of each of the characters or to hand down a sentence that fits their crime. Here guilt is an inner burden, and the suspense rests on whether or not they are able to free themselves from it.

Live Flesh was shot on location on the outskirts of Madrid, where slums and futuristic buildings sit side by side: 'You'd think you were in Sarajevo,' says Clara when she discovers Victor's hovel. It is also one of Almodóvar's few films to take account of the political changes in Spanish society. The circular structure of the screenplay, which begins and ends with a woman giving birth, allows us to measure the road travelled in barely twenty-five years. Victor is born amid streets made deserted by fear; his son enters the world in a Madrid whose pavements are teeming with people.

Live Flesh still stands by itself in Almodóvar's filmography. Although it has been assimilated to the point where it is almost unrecognizable, this film has digested what is essentially foreign material, while remaining faithful to the rules of its genre — the thriller — without using comedy or melodrama for contrast. Almodóvar has also found a balance between male and female, creating a common space for actors and actresses of very different kinds. This excursion to the borders of his world, and even a little beyond them, is fascinating to watch.

Live Flesh – a thriller

After the historic prologue of *Live Flesh*, a virtuoso sequence makes it clear that the film belongs firmly in its genre – the thriller.

Victor is trying to forget the disappointment that Helena, a rich heroin addict, has inflicted on him, by taking a bus ride (it's his fate, he was born on a bus), when he sees the young woman on her balcony, in a precise long shot that is very much Hitchcock. We then move to the interior of the flat, where Helena is reading the tarot cards (because her fate has yet to be decided), while she waits for her dealer. When the bell rings, she's confused and lets Victor in.

He enters the luxurious flat, seen in a panoramic shot that ends with Victor standing in the centre of a carpet with a pattern of concentric circles. He's the object, the target. When Helena realizes her mistake, there begins a dialogue typical of Almodóvar, in which the desire of one character collides with the contempt and lack of understanding of the other.

Helena goes to her bedroom to look for a gun, and Almodóvar places in the bottom left-hand corner of the frame the bluish screen of a TV set on which Buñuel's *The Criminal Life of Archibaldo de la Cruz* is showing. Victor is humiliated by Helena, they fight and she passes out, and all this is closely interwoven with the story of Archibaldo's first crime, which assumes increasing importance until it occupies the whole screen. This is no mere quotation, still less a wink to the audience – it's a form of perfectly mastered collage. In his early films, Almodóvar rejected his inheritance from Buñuél, but now he felt he was in a position to be able to use the old master's art openly.

This piece of counterpoint marks a first pause, during which David and Sancho, two police officers called out by a neighbour, arrive. We then return to Victor, who is waiting for Helena to wake up, while Archibaldo's criminal career continues to unfold on the TV screen (now we're at the sequence where he drags along a shop dummy as if it were a corpse). The film's first climax, which will establish the pattern of the tragedies to come, is now set up. Through the window, the police officers see Victor attacking Helena, whereas in fact it is the junkie who has attacked the young man because he sent her supplier away.

As they go up the stairs, the two policemen are filmed like shadow puppets, as in a thriller from the 1930s. But when they enter the flat and Victor takes Helena hostage, we're truly in the cinema of Almodóvar: the situation begins to get out of hand and transgression takes over. The dialogue between Victor and Sancho, the old cop, is a cruel satire on Spanish machismo. (On that subject, Almodóvar told Frédéric Strauss: 'The word *huevos* [which means both "eggs" and "balls"] forms half the vocabulary of Spanish men.')

David, the younger officer, aims at his colleague instead of at the suspect, and when he persuades Victor to let Helena go, the play of expressions and the physical communication between the cop and the heroin addict is like a bullfighter's pass with the cape, just before his final thrust of the sword, filmed in slow motion.

Liberto Rabal, Francesca Neri and Javier Bardem in *Live Flesh* (1997).

Eloy Azorínin in
All About My Mother (1999).

Trophies

Since then, Almodóvar has made a film every two years. Early in 1998, he started work on *All About My Mother*, taking care to let people in Madrid know he was about to be disloyal to them by setting the greater part of his story in Barcelona. The cast included Marisa Paredes, Penélope Cruz and Cecilia Roth. Following a period of exile in Madrid, Roth had returned to her native Argentina, from where Almodóvar summoned her back. He wanted to turn her into a mother of a kind never seen before in his films. His previous maternal figures were all based — even if by contrast — on Francesca Caballero. She was ill, and died in September 1999, a few months after the film was released. This time, as he explained to Frédéric Strauss, Almodóvar wanted a modern, educated mother, bringing up her son alone.

He made the character of Manuela a nurse, and at the beginning of the film he reintroduced a motif he had already used in *The Flower of My Secret*. Manuela (Cecilia Roth) heads a medical team responsible for removing the organs of patients who 69

have been declared clinically dead, and therefore charged with persuading relatives to authorize their removal. While the prologue of *The Flower of My Secret* ends with our suddenly discovering that the discussion between the doctors and a 'patient' is for training purposes, this time the scene – in which Manuela plays the widow of a man killed in an accident – is tragically premonitory.

Esteban, the adored son endowed with every gift, will shortly die, knocked down by a car as he is running after the taxi of Huma Rojo (Marisa Paredes), a star whose autograph he is trying to get. The film never puts itself at a distance from pain, and here Almodóvar, who has so often toyed with melodrama, throws himself into it without restraint. The figures who gather around Manuela after her son's death are all of a nature to arouse compassion, and soften the stoniest heart. The nurse leaves for Barcelona

to keep the promise she had made to Esteban, that she would find his father, a transvestite called Lola. The world of drug-dealing and prostitution, so often depicted with energy and humour, is shown this time as a hell visited by two angels, Manuela and Rosa (Penélope Cruz), a nun who devotes herself to helping transvestites. As he will demonstrate again in *Volver*, Pedro Almodóvar sees Penélope Cruz only as a mother, and after making her give birth on public transport, he now makes her carry Lola's child (and his HIV), Lola himself having run off.

Punctuated by titles that mark the passage of time (two and a half years pass in ninety minutes), Manuela's grief is gradually replaced by her will to live. The story has two recurring points of reference, Joseph L. Mankiewicz's *Eve* and Tennessee Williams's *A Streetcar Named Desire*. It is fluid and – once we accept the idea of a father who is a transvestite, a

stumbling-block for some American critics — made in a traditional style. So much so that one hardly notices its formal daring, such as the cruel and harrowing way in which Almodóvar makes Cecilia Roth tell the story of Esteban's death over and over again, weeping every time, or the inclusion of an alien element, the spectacle of the transsexual Antonia San Juan.

All About My Mother was the first of Pedro Almodóvar's films to be selected for the Cannes Film Festival, in 1999. France has a curious relationship with him; it ignored him longer than other countries did (New York honoured him well before Paris), and in 1985 he publicly accused the Cannes selectors of ignoring Spanish cinema. But since Women on the Verge of a Nervous Breakdown, French audiences have stuck by him. Ciby 2000 has produced four of his films and after the Bouygues group closed the company down, Renn Productions, owned by Claude Berri, who co-financed All About My Mother, took over. At Cannes, press and gala performances were greeted with enthusiasm, but the jury, chaired by David Cronenberg, awarded the Palme d'or to Rosetta, by the Dardenne brothers, and Almodóvar had to be content with the prize for best director. His pride was so wounded (he publicly accused Cronenberg of acting out of jealousy) that three years later he chose to show Talk to Her at the Paris Film Festival, rather than at the Palais des Festivals in Cannes.

But that snub did nothing to mar the film's tremendous success, first in Spain, then all over the world, and on 26 March 2000 it won the Oscar for best foreign film. Hollywood again made eyes at the boy from Calzada de Calatrava, and another project, an adaptation of Pete Dexter's The Paperboy, a story of initiation set in Miami, was officially announced.

Above: Candela Peña in All About My Mother (1999).

Right: Pedro Almodóvar with Antonia San Juan on the set of All About My Mother (1999).

Following pages: Lluís Pasqual and Marisa Paredes in All About My Mother (1999).

'My mother's last dream', by Pedro Almodóvar Caballero

Last Saturday, when I went out of the house, I found that it was a beautiful sunny day. It was the first sunny day without my mother. I wept behind my glasses, and I would weep a lot that day. I hadn't slept the night before, and I walked around like an orphan, looking for a taxi to take me to the Funérarium del Sud.

I'm not a great one for cemetery visits and other rituals, but my mother is an essential figure in my life. For the name I use in public, I've never added her surname to my father's, as is the custom in Spain, and as she would have wished. 'Your name's Pedro Almódovar Caballero. Who's this Almódovar fellow?', she asked me one day, and she was almost angry with me.

People think children belong to a certain time. But it lasts. A long time. A very long time. That's what Lorca used to say. And mothers don't belong to a certain time, either. And they don't need anything special to be essential, important, unforgettable, and to be teachers. Mothers can withstand anything. I learned a lot from my mother, without either of us realizing it. I learned something that was vital for my work, the difference between fiction and reality, and how reality needs to be complemented by fiction to make life easier.

I have memories of my mother at all the different periods of her life. The most epic part, perhaps, is the time she spent in a village in Badajoz, Orellana la Vieja, the bridge between the two great worlds where I lived before I was swallowed up by Madrid: La Mancha and Extremadura. Although my sisters don't like me to talk about it, when we first lived there, our financial situation was precarious. My mother was always very creative, I've never known anyone as inventive. In La Mancha, they say of a person like her, 'She can get milk from an oil can.' There was no electricity in the street where we lived, it was a dirt road, impossible to keep clean, and it turned into mud in the rain. The street was at the end of the village, and had been built on ground that was full of pieces of slate. I don't know how the girls walked on those sharp stones in high heels. To me, it wasn't a street, it reminded me more of a Western. Living there was hard but it was cheap, and our neighbours were wonderful people and very hospitable. And they were illiterate, too.

To supplement my father's wages, my mother set up a business reading and writing letters, as in the film *Central do Brasil*. I was eight; usually, it would be me who wrote the letters and she who read the ones our neighbours received. Often, as I listened to what my mother was reading, I would notice to my amazement that it didn't correspond exactly to what was written on the paper: she would invent some of it. The neighbours didn't know, because what she invented was always an enhancement of their lives and they came away from the reading delighted. Having seen clearly that my mother never kept to the original text, when we got home one day, I told her off about it. I said, 'Why did you read that he's always thinking of his grandmother and that he feels nostalgic about the time when she used to cut his hair on the doorstep, in front of the washbasin? The letter doesn't even mention his grandmother.' And she said, 'But did you see how happy she was?'

She was right. My mother filled in the gaps in the letters, she told the neighbours the things they wanted to hear, sometimes things the writer had probably forgotten but would have been quite happy to have written. These improvisations held an important lesson for me. They established the difference between fiction and reality, they showed me how reality needs fiction to be complete, more pleasant, more endurable ...

Although I was exhausted from making promotional trips (*All About My Mother* was then being released worldwide and it was a matter of chance that I decided to dedicate the film to her, as a mother and as an actress; I was very hesitant, because I wasn't sure if she liked my films), luckily I was with her in Madrid. All four of us were with her. Two hours before the 'crucial moment', Agustín and I came to see her for the half-hour visit that was allowed in the intensive care unit, while my sisters waited for their turn.

My mother was asleep. We woke her up. Her dream must have been so pleasant and absorbing that it hadn't really left her, although she spoke to us quite lucidly. She asked us if there was a thunderstorm at that moment, and we said no. We asked her how she felt and she said she felt fine. She asked Agustín about his children, who had just come back from holiday. Agustín told her he had them with him for the weekend and that they would eat together. My mother asked him if he had shopped for their food, and my brother said yes. I told her I had to go to Italy to promote my film, but I'd stay in Madrid if she wanted me to. She told me to go, and to do whatever I needed to do. What bothered her about this trip was Agustín's children. She asked, 'And the children, who's going to take care of them?' Agustín said he wasn't going with me, and would stay. She was pleased about that.

A nurse came in, and said our visiting time was up, and told my mother they were going to bring her something to eat. My mother said, 'The food won't weigh my body down very much.' I found that answer sweet and strange. Three hours later, she died. Of everything she said to us during that last visit, it's her question about the storm that stays with me. That Friday was a sunny day, and some of the sunshine came in through the window. What storm was my mother thinking about in her last dream?

This is an extract from an article published in *El País*, 14 September 1999.

Between life and death

In spring 2000, the Oscar-winner returned to Spain. He had given up the idea of filming far from home and was hesitating between two projects. The first was the story of a transvestite, a former pupil at a religious boarding school. Almodóvar had been working on this idea — unless it was the other way round — for almost ten years. Now he was looking for his leading actor, and he 'cross-dressed' all the handsome young actors of the Spanish-speaking world. Later, he gave *El País* a photograph of Eduardo Noriega, praying and wearing a mantilla. But for the moment things didn't work out. He had already written another screenplay, and *that* was the one he turned into a film.

Talk to Her fits alongside *The Flower of My Secret* and *All About My Mother*: it deals with mourning and loss, of births that heal wounds, of creation and sacrifices. Yet the story is formally much bolder, its chronology is not linear, and in the middle of the film there is a silent short, *The Shrinking Lover*. The command of the title is addressed to its two male characters, Benigno (Javier Cámara, a TV actor) and Marco (the Argentine actor Dario Grandinetti). After sitting next to each other at a performance by the dancer and choreographer Pina Bausch, the two men meet again in a clinic where Benigno is a nurse. Marco has come to sit alongside Lydia (Rosario Flores), his partner, a bullfighter who has been in a coma since being injured during a fight (*lidia*, in Spanish). Benigno is nursing Alicia, a dancer, who is also unconscious.

While Marco's ties to his lover and to life itself are loosening, Benigno has become so strongly attracted to Alicia that he rapes her while unconscious, making her pregnant. (Almodóvar based this on an incident that took place in New York.) In this tale organized on the principle of the arbitrary nature of life (Lydia consciously ran a risk, but Alicia's accident could not have been foreseen), art offers a refuge to the two main characters: Pina Bausch's dancing, the music of Caetano Veloso, whom we see and hear singing 'Curucucu Paloma', and lastly, *The Shrinking Lover*, a silent Spanish film that never existed. This short film shows a man exploring a gigantic female body, slipping between the thighs of a woman whose head we never see, and entering her open vagina with his whole body. This is not the first time a man finds his head between a woman's legs in an Almodóvar film — think of Miguel Bosé and Victoria Abril in *High Heels* and Javier Bardem and Francesca Neri in

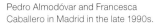

Pedro Almodóvar and Francesca Caballero in Madrid in the late 1990s.

Rosario Flores in *Talk to Her* (2002).

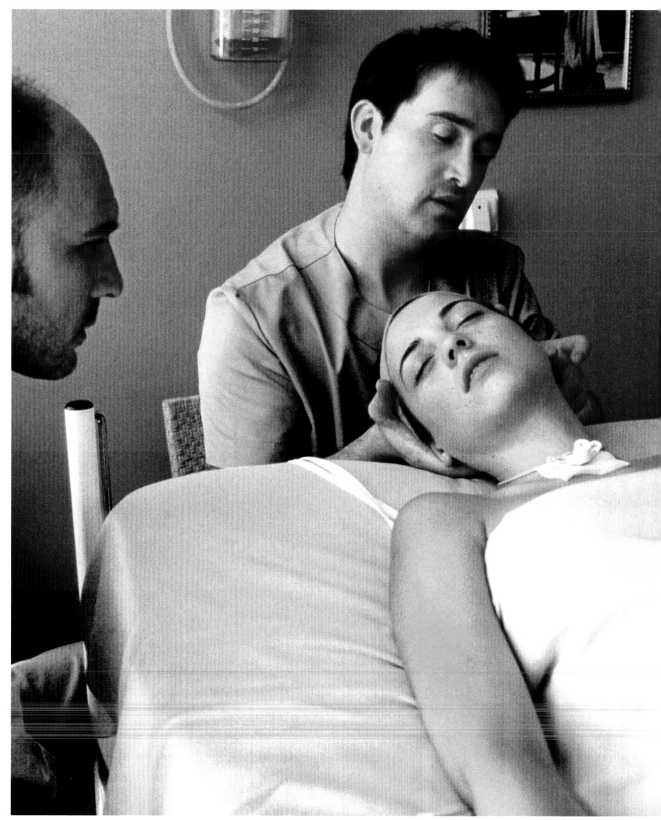

Improving on reality

From the time when he made films in Super 8 and spoke his commentary during the projection, Pedro Almodóvar was already obsessed by the need to tell a story. This desire to retain a basic role for narrative was for a time obscured by the joyful anarchy of his early films and the increase in the number of his characters. In November 1982 he confessed to *La Revista de cine* that he was incapable of having only two main characters, 'and of getting to the bottom of things'. That does not mean that he limited himself to drawing cardboard figures. Two years after the release of *Pepi, Luci, Bom and Other Girls on the Heap*, Almodóvar wrote for the newsletter of the Alphaville cinemas a detailed biography of each of his heroines, tracing their family tree, and their geographical and professional histories. He says that his fascination with fiction dates back to the time when his mother read their letters to her illiterate neighbours in the little village in Extremadura where the family had settled. This way of embellishing reality seemed to him a way of making it more bearable. In the course of interviews, he has revealed some of his autobiographical sources: formative episodes from his childhood, as well as from his adult life. When *Law of Desire* was released, he admitted that the way Pablo Quintero, the film director played by Eusebio Poncela, writes the letter he would have liked to receive and sends this ideal letter to his lover, almost happened to him, but he stopped short of sending it.

His material can have sources other than personal experience. Almodóvar – who has considered turning Jean Cocteau's *La Voix humaine* into a film – has made only one adaptation, using a novel by Ruth Rendell (Claude Chabrol's favourite writer) as the basis for *Live Flesh*. On the contrary, he likes to draw inspiration from current events. When he was embarking on *Volver*, there was a news item from Puerto Rico – a man separated from his wife, whose family were preventing him seeing her, killed his mother-in-law so that he could see his wife at the funeral. Nothing remains of this anecdote in the final screenplay, through a process of distillation that preserves some of its mystery. Only some of its mystery, because Pedro Almodóvar is probably the sole director to have devoted a whole film to the transformation of memory in fiction. *Bad Education* is, among many other things, an account of the birth of a story. It had a particularly long gestation because Almodóvar had written a short story entitled 'The Visit' about ten years before work started on the film. This story about a pupil's return to his religious boarding school is at the centre of the film as it was made, but it is then used as the material of fiction, since the character Ángel offers it to the director Enrique Goded, so that he can turn it into a screenplay (we've seen him at the beginning of the film, short of inspiration and cutting out ridiculous news items from the papers in the hope of finding an idea).

Pedro Almodóvar in 1991.

Javier Cámara, Dario Grandinetti and Leonor Watling in *Talk to Her* (2002).

Live Flesh — but here, Almodóvar takes the impulse to its logical conclusion. In another sense, the little human being who will finally emerge from Alicia's body brings her back to the world of the living.

The softness of Javier Aguirresarobe's images and the melancholy grace of Alberto Iglesias's score together make *Talk to Her* a film whose daring is hidden behind a gentle sweetness. Once again, Almodóvar has made use of melodramatic devices, far-fetched situations and exaggerated emotions, polishing and burnishing them in his elegant handling of chronology, and allowing them to resonate in the creative presence of major artists like Bausch and Veloso. It is still collage, as in the period of *Labyrinth of Passion*, but it all fits together harmoniously and you can't even guess where the joins occur. *Talk to Her* was greeted enthusiastically in the United States, and this time Almodóvar left Los Angeles with the Oscar for best screenplay.

The same passion

The Mexican actor Gael García Bernal fitted the bill, and he played the central character in *Bad Education*. He adopted a Spanish accent, dressed in drag and carried all the sins of the film on his shoulders — not to mention that his relationship with his director was terrible. The tangled web of heterosexual desire and the convoluted plot of *Talk to Her* gave way to an exclusively male world, made up of the layers of a past that the screenplay of *Bad Education* painstakingly uncovers. The film begins in 1980, when we meet a young filmmaker, Enrique Goded, played by Fele Martínez, who looks a little like Eusebio Poncela (Pablo Quintero in *Law of Desire*), with his delicate features and clear gaze. Goded is looking for an idea for his next film.

Providence brings to his door a young man claiming to be Ignacio, Enrique's lover when he was young, who is carrying under his arm a story, *The Visit*, which describes a transvestite's return to the boarding school where he was raped by a priest. In the real world (if it exists and after seeing *Bad Education* we may well doubt it), *The Visit* is the first version of the screenplay of the film, as Almodóvar wrote it in the early 1990s. There then begins a sordid process of bargaining between Goded and the pseudo-Ignacio, the former wishing to get his hands on the story (a situation in which Almodóvar, who has always written his own screenplays, has never found himself), and the latter coveting the leading role.

This was not the first time that Almodóvar had reflected on the price one has to pay to be creative, but he had never done so with such chilly lucidity. Enrique Goded does not attract our sympathy, and that is of no concern to him. The last shot of the film shows him alone, leaning against a metal gate, and a title informs us that since the story took place, he has continued to make films with the same passion.

This passion for the cinema is the only form of redemption that we glimpse in *Bad Education*. In certain respects it is the most American of Almodóvar's films, since it shows desire leading only to unhappiness and death. But there are still the films: we see Ignacio and Enrique as children fleeing the advances of Father Manolo in the darkness of the village cinema, and watching spellbound a melodrama starring Sara Montiel, *Esa Mujer*, by Mario Camus (1968). Other people's films have

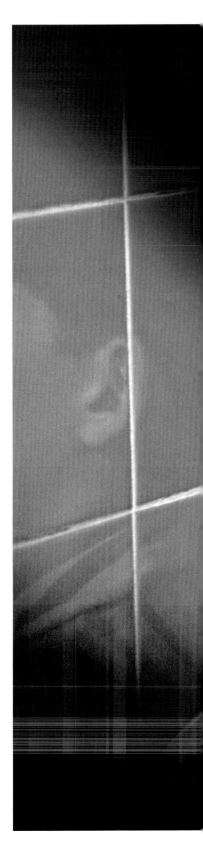

Nacho Pérez and Raúl García Forneiro in *Bad Education* (2004).

Following pages: Nacho Pérez and Daniel Giménez Cacho in *Bad Education* (2004).

Pedro Almodóvar and Gael García Bernal in *Bad Education* (2004).

long had their place in those of Almodóvar. These cinematic references may be narrated — in *High Heels*, Rebeca compares her relationship with her mother with the conflict between Ingrid Bergman and Liv Ullmann in Ingmar Bergman's *Autumn Sonata* — or shown on screen: Buñuel's *The Criminal Life of Archibaldo de la Cruz* in *Live Flesh*, Mankiewicz's *Eve* in *All About My Mother*. They are no longer simply references, or winks to the audience, but elements of the reality in which the characters are living. At the end of *Bad Education*, two killers are passing the time, waiting to commit their crime. There's a festival

of crime films on, and they take the opportunity to see Marcel Carné's *Thérèse Raquin*, Billy Wilder's *Double Indemnity* or Jean Renoir's *La Bête humaine* (we don't know which, because we only see the posters). 'You'd think all these films were about us,' says one of the murderous cinema-goers, as they emerge from the darkness.

Bad Education opened the Cannes Film Festival, out of competition, and Almodóvar spent much of his time there explaining that he had not been trying to take revenge on the priests and that *Bad Education* was no more anticlerical a film than *Dark Habits*.

A memory and three productions –
Dark Habits, Law of Desire, Bad Education

The day on which Almodóvar had to sing a romantic ballad with ambiguous new words to the Father Superior of his boarding school inspired him three times over. The Mother Superior of *Dark Habits* is lost in adoration in the presence of Yolanda Bell, the bolero singer who decides, on the convent's feast day, to sing her a refrain with cruel words. There follow a series of ironic shots showing Yolanda miming erotic movements, some tender close-ups of the transfigured face of the Mother Superior (Julieta Serrano) and some very joyful wide-angle shots of the three nuns accompanying the singer: Carmen Maura on the bongos, Marisa Paredes on bass and Chus Lampreave singing. In *Law of Desire*, Tina (Carmen Maura) walks with her daughter Ada past the chapel of the boarding school where she studied when she was a little boy. She goes inside the shadowy chapel, hears someone playing a canticle to the Virgin on the organ and starts singing it. She approaches the priest who is at the keyboard, a handsome man of around sixty. A very simple sequence of shots and reverse shots of the faces of the former pupil and his spiritual director present a dialogue of great dramatic intensity, in which information tumbles out ('I have only loved two men, you, my spiritual director, and my father, and you both abandoned me,' says Tina) and bitterness boils up.

The tension is hardly relaxed by an absurd line of dialogue of the sort Almodóvar likes so much: 'How you've changed,' says the priest in astonishment, when he learns that the woman who has just spoken to him is his former pupil. 'I'm still the same,' Tina replies, bringing the scene back into the vein of tragedy. She is eventually thrown out by the man of the cloth, who advises her to flee from her memories as he has fled from his. As she leaves, the sound of the organ is drowned out by the plastic harmonica that Pablo (Tina's brother, a film director) has given Ada.

Finally, the anecdote is filmed in *Bad Education* just as the director had described it twenty years earlier. An overweight priest, terrifying and repulsive, snatches little Ignacio away from his friends and takes him to the Father Superior so that he can sing his praises as the gardener whose job is to 'brighten the colours of the flowers the Lord has entrusted to him'. The central figure in the sequence is not the person to whom the memory belongs, a child with innocent gestures (in contrast with Yolanda Bell's suggestive pouting), but Father Manolo (Daniel Giménez Cacho), around whom the camera moves very softly, showing the complexity of the impulses and emotions that are racking the body and soul under the cassock. He is both the counterpart of the monster devoid of compassion of *Law of Desire*, and the companion in suffering of the Mother Superior of the Humiliated Sisters of Redemption.

Right:
Cecilia Roth in *Dark Habits* (1983).

Below, left:
Carmen Maura and Germán Cobos in *Law of Desire* (1987).

Below, right: Nacho Pérez (right) in *Bad Education* (2004).

Coming back, and leaving again

After this perilous excursion into the past, it is time to come back. To the village, to women, to the actresses who have stayed with him through the quarter-century that has passed since *Pepi, Luci, Bom and Other Girls on the Heap*. So the film will be called *Volver*, meaning 'to come back'. It begins in a cemetery in La Mancha, where the women are sweeping the gravestones on a very windy day. It was a situation that filled the teenage Pedro with such horror that he had to leave for Madrid, but which he now considers a fascinating, comforting ritual.

It's a return to the village, then, but also to the interiors of the cheap blocks of flats on the outskirts of Madrid. That's where Raimunda (Penélope Cruz) lives with her daughter Paula (Yohana Cobo) and her good-for-nothing husband. How he comes to disappear into the bowels of a freezer, how, in Raimunda's home village, Irene, her dead mother, reappears with the features of Carmen Maura, how all these women learn to live together, without worrying about the boundaries between life and death, the city and the country, as long as they don't have to put up with men, is the whole story of *Volver*.

This revisiting of Almodóvar's past – his childhood in La Mancha, obviously, but also his early films – is done with the assurance of a man who has travelled a long way, and who for the first time in many years can allow himself to slip a scatological gag into his script without its appearing to break the tone, since, as both screenwriter and director, he is in full control of tone and register. He makes his stars shine, giving Penélope Cruz the maternal sensuality of an Italian star of the 1950s, and finding again with Carmen Maura a closeness that had survived an estrangement of seventeen years.

For all that, *Volver* is not a light film. Its central theme is death and absence, especially that of Francesca Caballero. In the production notes, Almodóvar describes the shoot as a 'second, painless mourning'. It is also a kind of gravestone over his career.

In any case, this is what he said in January 2007 in an interview he gave to *El País*. *Volver* had just received five Goyas, enough to compensate for previous disappointments; at Cannes, where it was presented in competition, it had received only the prize for best screenplay, and a joint prize for the actresses; at the Oscars, where it had not been nominated

in the 'best foreign film category', Penélope Cruz missed the prize for best actress. Always sensitive on the matter of honours, Almodóvar admits that this was like a 'cold shower'. And he described the film as follows: '[*Volver* is] the last in the line of films that I have made about the world of women, and a type of family that has moved from the country-side to the capital in search of fortune. And, yes, it marks the end of a cycle. Today I feel I am on the edge of other abysses.'

Almodóvar then mentions a film with Penélope Cruz, *La Piel que habito* ('The skin in which I live'), whose subject is revenge, an entirely different ap-proach to the manipulation of images. He says in passing, 'For the first time I talked to someone about sharing my writing and my world.' He is allowing himself to think about historical films, inspired by nineteenth-century Spanish literature or by Franco and the Civil War. 'I believe enough time has passed for us to talk about this subject naturally.' Finally he has bought the film rights to *Decidme cómo es un árbol* ('Tell me what a tree is like'), the memoirs of the Communist poet and militant Marcos Ana, who was imprisoned in one of Franco's jails at the age of nineteen and released twenty years later.

Finally, Almodóvar isn't taking a leap in the dark, but going back to what he has done before. In the spring of 2008, he began shooting *Broken Embraces*. At the customary press conference that he gave on that occasion, he presented the film as a 'celebration of fiction', a 'feast for a storyteller'. He

could have been a bit more precise, and said, 'the film will be a celebration of cinema, a feast of writ-ing for the screen.'

In terms of the number of sets, the size of the budget and the time it took to shoot it, *Broken Embraces* was the biggest production undertaken by El Deseo. The press were barred from the set, and a few weeks before it was released, Almodóvar even indulged himself by pulling the wool over the eyes of his audiences. While filming *Broken Embraces*, he had made a humorous and 'sloppy' (as he said him-self) short film, under the pseudonym Mateo Blanco, shown on 13 February 2009 on Canal Plus Spain. *La Concejala antropófaga* ('The Man-eating Councillor') is about a female conservative town councillor, a cocaine addict and sex maniac. So this little film harked back to the excesses of the Movida, and some people started to imagine that the 'provocateur' of *Pepi, Luci, Bom and Other Girls on the Heap* was back.

They were to be disappointed. In keeping with a ritual that had started with *Volver*, *Broken Embraces* came out in Spain in the spring, on 18 March 2009, before being presented in competition at Cannes in May. This time things didn't go nearly as well. Spanish reviews were very lukewarm. *El País*, which had done so much to help build Almodóvar's reputation when Diego Galán was its film critic, published a violent piece by Carlos Boyero, one of a group of deliberate iconoclasts, who had already had Spanish filmmak-ers up in arms. More seriously, *Broken Embraces* was much less successful with the public than *Volver*.

Nobody was expecting a film like this. Mass audiences who had enjoyed the director's tales of family life, especially *All About my Mother* and *Volver*, were now being offered a sophisticated film noir. And loyal fans hoping to see fulfilled the promise of a leap into the unknown found a film that resembles a long flashback. A few months later, people realized that Almodóvar had followed the same path as another director, his almost exact contemporary, Jim Jarmusch. He too had gone back over old ground in *The Limits of Control* (2009), which presents again some figures familiar from his earlier work, in an attempt to give them a sense of movement that had been lost with the passage of time. The directors who belong to the last generation of auteur cinema, that of Almodóvar, Nanni Moretti and Jarmusch, have no heirs. The

Opposite page, left: Carmen Maura and Penélope Cruz in *Volver* (2006).

Opposite page, right: Pedro Almodóvar with Lola Dueñas, Penélope Cruz and Chus Lampreave, on the set of *Volver* (2006).

Below: the women from La Mancha in *Volver* (2006).

Lluís Homar and Penélope Cruz in *Broken Embraces* (2009).

cinema in which they were born and grew up is dead, and the directors of the third millennium do not attain (nor do they claim to do so) the stature of major artist, which Almodóvar's generation inherited from the likes of Bergman, Truffaut and Scorsese. The sense of uncertainty resulting from this change is perceptible in many films made in the 1990s, and Almodóvar has the flair to give it supremely elegant shape.

The broken embrace of the film's title is the one that brought together, in the 1980s, Mateo (Lluís Homar) and Lena (Penélope Cruz), a film director and his leading actress. Twenty-five years later, Mateo has lost everything — Lena, his sight, films, even his own name. Now blind, he writes screenplays under the name Harry Caine. The film goes back and forth between past and present, losing itself voluptuously in the convolutions of the plot. The characters are both typical figures from Almodóvar's world and archetypes of cinema history: Penélope Cruz is a poor young girl who becomes an actress under the protection of one of those financial wizards who emerged under the Socialist government of Felipe González. This man's son wants to be a film director.

Below: Lluís Homar and Penélope Cruz in *Broken Embraces* (2009).

Opposite page: Tamar Novas, Blanca Portillo and Lluís Homar in *Broken Embraces* (2009).

Following pages: Penélope Cruz in *Broken Embraces* (2009).

Given the job of filming — in video — *Chicas y Maletas* ('Girls and Suitcases'), the film that Lena is shooting under Mateo's direction, he falls madly in love with him. This is only one of the countless games the film plays with the audience, making it turn giddy, not to say sea-sick.

In *Broken Embraces*, Almodóvar handles cinema in the way he handled the family in *Volver*. He goes back over all his previous experiments, studying them, rearranging them and putting them in perspective. In order to construct this monument to cinema, he calls upon innumerable directors. Some, like Luis Buñuel and Douglas Sirk, had already made their appearance in his films. Others, such as Michelangelo Antonioni or Roberto Rossellini, appear for the first time. Not forgetting Pedro Almodóvar, who now comes to his own rescue. The sequence from *Chicas y Maletas* that we see is in fact an excerpt from *Women on the Verge of a Nervous Breakdown*.

To help audiences (and journalists) find their way through the intricacies of this splicing together (a method he has always liked), Almodóvar wrote the press release for *Broken Embraces* himself. This document is usually a guide intended for journalists who aren't necessarily on the ball, written in an all-purpose style. This one was almost a manifesto. Almodóvar lists every single thing he is trying to do, explains every reference and draws attention to a particular sequence: the scene in which Lena falls downstairs is associated in his mind with John M. Stahl's *Leave Her to Heaven* (1945) starring Gene Tierney, and with Buñuel's El (1952). Almodóvar dwells at length on the distinction he makes between his homages to the directors he loves, and his use of extracts from their films. 'I don't make films "in the style of …", he says.

Returning to his previous experiments in using extracts or fragments of dialogue from film classics (Nicholas Ray's *Johnny Guitar* in *Women on the Verge of a Nervous Breakdown*, or Ingmar Bergman's *Cries and Whispers* in *High Heels*), he makes the point that when he was making them, these sequences had a place in the story and dramatic structure of his films. In *Broken Embraces*, we see Lena watching Rossellini's *Voyage to Italy* (1953), then shooting a sequence from *Women on the Verge of a Nervous Breakdown*. In addition to these explicit references, there are others, hidden or obvious, in almost every shot. 'This is the first time that I have made so explicit a declaration of love for cinema, not in a specific sequence but throughout a whole film,' he ends by confessing.

It is a brilliant film, and Almodóvar's comments are brilliant. But this intoxication with his mastery of cinema, his ability to invoke its tutelary deities, carries its own risk of suffering a hangover. *Volver* and *Broken Embraces* are like a magnificent way of summing up an oeuvre. But in the latter, we can detect a feverish anxiety. The figure of the blind film director (which Woody Allen had used shortly before he decided to leave Manhattan, in his *Hollywood Ending* of 2002) suggests, if not a kind of impotence, then at least a fear of it. This expressed itself more crudely in the dispute in which Almodóvar engaged with *El País* when he speculated publicly whether the paper 'could not afford to find somebody else' (i.e. other than Carlos Boyero) to cover the Cannes Festival. This bitter disappointment at the loss of the cinephile world in which they had blossomed is shared very widely among directors of Almodóvar's generation. His ubiquity in the magazine press — he has shared (false) confidences about his private life with readers of *Vanity Fair* — and his readiness to engage in spectacular controversies (he attacked Pope Benedict XVI on the subject of the family, provoking an official response from the Vatican) may also be seen as attempts to counteract the bad reception that awaited *Broken Embraces* as it was released all over the world.

In 2010 Almodóvar will shoot *La Piel que habito*, based on Thierry Jonquet's 1999 novel, *Mygale*. Almodóvar himself has described it as a 'horror film with no screams or fear', adding that Penélope Cruz will not appear in it, but that Antonio Banderas is exactly the right age, at fifty, to play a psychopath. And sixty's a good age for a director who still wishes to fascinate and surprise us.

Chronology

1951
25 September. Birth of Pedro Almodóvar at Calzada de Calatrava Ciudad Real, La Mancha). Sources prior to 1990 – the biography by Boquerini and the dictionary *Cine Español* published in 1989 by the Ministry of Culture – give the date as 1949.

1960
The Almodóvar family, who had left La Mancha for Extremadura, send Pedro to the Salesian Fathers' school in Cáceres.

1967
Pedro leaves for Madrid. The first art and experimental cinemas open in the capital.

1969
He obtains an administrative job with Telefónica, which he will keep for over ten years.

1970
He meets the underground theatre group, Los Goliardos, its director, Félix Rotaeta, who will be his actor and producer, and one of the actresses, Carmen Maura.

1971
Closure of the state cinema school, which only reopened after the death of Franco.

1972
Agustín Almodóvar, called Tinín, joins him in Madrid.

1974
He shoots first short films in Super 8.

1977
General elections in Spain. Almodóvar starts writing *Erecciones generales* with the idea of turning it into a photo-novel. **11 November.** Royal decree 3.071 ends film censorship, introduced by Franco.

1978
Makes *Folle … Folle … Fólleme Tim!*, a feature film in Super 8, and *Salomé*, his first film in 16mm, with professional actors.

1979
June. Decides to make *Erecciones generales* as a film, and shoots the first forty-five minutes.

1980
June. Finishes shooting *Erecciones*, now titled *Pepi, Luci, Bom and Other Girls on the Heap.* **27 October.** It opens in two Madrid cinemas, after being presented at San Sebastián in September.

1981
The Alphaville cinemas, temples of Madrid cinema, announce that they will co-produce Almodóvar's second feature film, *Labyrinth of Passion*.

1982
24 September. *Labyrinth of Passion* is shown at San Sebastián Festival. **October.** The filmmaker Pilar Miró is appointed 'director of cinema' when the Socialist Party wins the elections. She sets up a system of state aid to support film production.

1983
9 September. *Dark Habits*, shown out of competition at Venice, is enthusiastically received by the audience. **31 December.** Almodóvar gives a New Year concert at the Rock-Ola, a top venue for the Movida, with Fanny McNamara and Alaska.

1984
26 October. *What Have I Done to Deserve This?* opens in Madrid and has its New York premiere on 12 April.

1986
6 March. *Matador* opens in Madrid.

1987
7 February. *Law of Desire* is a triumph at the thirty-seventh Berlin Film Festival. **20 July.** 'Pedro Almodóvar Square' is named in Calzada de Calatrava, in the presence of a distinguished gathering. *What Have I Done to Deserve This?* is shown at the event. **November.** *Women on the Verge of a Nervous Breakdown* is shot in Madrid.

1989
6 February. *Women on the Verge of a Nervous Breakdown* receives sixteen nominations at the Goyas, out of a possible eighteen. The film wins five awards and is nominated for an Oscar for best foreign film. **29 March.** A public row between Pedro Almodóvar and Carmen Maura at the Oscars in Los Angeles.

1990
22 January. First showing of *Tie Me Up! Tie Me Down!* at the Fuencarral cinema in Madrid, in the presence of the Minister of Culture, Jorge Semprún, and other dignitaries. **11 February.** Presentation of the film in Berlin, where it is well received. **April.** Miramax, the American distributor of *Tie Me Up! Tie Me Down!*, opens an unsuccessful campaign, with Almodóvar, to stop the film being given an 'X' certificate. **26 November.** Antonio Banderas announces that he does not wish to play the lead in *High Heels*, and goes to Hollywood. The start of filming is postponed.

1991
16 February. Almodóvar announces he has replaced Antonio Banderas with Miguel Bosé. **23 October.** *High Heels* opens in Spain.

1992
May. For the first time, El Deseo produces a film not directed by Pedro Almodóvar, Alex de la Iglesia's *Acción mutante*. **August.** Almodóvar signs a petition in favour of a 'yes' vote to the Maastricht treaty, sponsored by the French Minister of Culture, Jack Lang.

1993
6 March. *High Heels* wins the César for best foreign film. **May.** Shooting starts on *Kika*, with a budget of 700 million pesetas. **29 October.** Release of *Kika*; damning review in *El País* the following day.

1994
April. The threat of an NC17 classification hanging over *Kika* in the United States leads Almodóvar to send an open letter to the American media, in which he says he is 'insulted' by this form of censorship. **November.** Two months before shooting starts on *The Flower of My Secret*, Ana Belén, who was to have played the lead, is replaced by Marisa Paredes.

The Almodóvar family in the 1950s.

Pedro Almodóvar and his parents in the 1950s.

Pedro Almodóvar in the 1960s.

Pedro and Agustín Almodóvar looking at a poster of Marilyn Monroe in 1975.

1995

February – April. Shooting *The Flower of My Secret* in Madrid. **18 September.** The film is presented at the San Sebastián Festival, first to the press, then to an audience of 3,000 people, who give it an ovation. Three days later, it opens in Spanish cinemas. **December.** *The Flower of My Secret* has attracted 920,000 viewers in Spain and taken over 500 million pesetas in receipts.

1996

26 July. Almodóvar and several other Spanish 88 directors react angrily to a speech by the Minister of Culture, a member of the recently elected Aznar government. The minister suggested that 'the last thirteen years [corresponding to the government of Felipe Gonzáles] were the worst in the history of Spanish cinema.' **7 August.** Summer re-release of *Dark Habits*.

1997

3 January. Filming of *Live Flesh* begins. Three weeks later, Liberto Rabal replaces Jorge Sanz in the role of Victor. **10 October.** Release of *Live Flesh* in Spain. **12 October.** Premiere at the New York Film Festival.

1998

September. Shooting of *All About My Mother* begins, with a budget of 700 million pesetas.

Pedro Almodóvar and Francesca Caballero in the late 1990s.

1999

8 April. Premiere of *All About My Mother* in Barcelona. **15 May.** The film is presented in competition at Cannes, a first for Almodóvar. **23 May.** The director received the prize for direction, the Palme d'or goes to the Dardenne brothers' *Rosetta*. **10 September.** Death of Francesca Caballero.

2000

29 January. *All About My Mother* wins seven Goyas. **17 February.** Wins the César for best foreign film. **26 March.** Takes the Oscar for best foreign film. **Autumn.** After giving screen tests to every young actor in Spain who might be suitable to play a drag role, Almodóvar abandons *Bad Education* for the time being and starts preparation of *Talk to Her*. **23 September.** Takes part in demonstrations against ETA terrorism.

2001

June. Shooting of *Talk to Her* begins at the Théâtre de la Ville, Paris, with the dance sequences choreographed by Pina Bausch. **July.** Bullfighting sequences provoke protests by organizations opposed to the *corrida*.

2002

6 February. Completion of post-production of *Talk to Her* announced by Almodóvar in an article in *El País*. **15 March.** The film is released in Spain. **18 September.** Almodóvar refuses to take part in the Marrakech Festival, which he describes as a 'Palace' event.

Miguel Bosé, Pedro Almodóvar and Victoria Abril on the set of *High Heels* (1991).

2003

February. Almodóvar plays an active part in protests against the American intervention in Iraq. **23 March.** He wins the Oscar for best original screenplay, for *Talk to Her*, in competition with the screenwriters of *Gangs of New York*, *Y tu mamá también*, *Far from Heaven* and *My Big Fat Greek Wedding*. But ignored at the Goyas. **16 June.** Shooting of *Bad Education* starts.

2004

14 March. Release of *Bad Education* in Spanish cinemas. **17 March.** José María Aznar's Partido Popular threatens to sue Almodóvar for defamation after he accuses it of trying to carry out a *coup d'état* in order to stay in power after the 11 March bomb attacks. He presents his excuses. **12 May.** *Bad Education*, presented out of competition, opens the fifty-eighth Cannes Film Festival.

2005

6 February. The Almodóvar brothers resign from the Spanish cinema academy that awards the Goyas in protest against its voting system. They return two years later, after the system is reformed. **18 July.** Shooting starts on *Volver*, which Almodóvar describes as 'a film a bit like *Indiana Jones*, but about domestic adventures'.

2006

17 March. Release of *Volver* in Spain after a preview at Puertollano, in La Mancha. **April.** Exhibition (*¡Almodóvar Exhibition!*) at the Cinémathèque française, in Paris. **18 May.** *Volver* is shown in competition at Cannes. The jury chaired by Wong Kar-wai awards a joint prize to its actresses, and the film wins the prize for best screenplay. **19 October.** Crown Prince Felipe awards Almodóvar the Prince of Asturias arts prize.

2007

28 January. *Volver* wins five Goyas.

2008

17 February. Almodóvar announces that he has bought the rights to *Decidme cómo es un árbol*, the autobiography of the Communist poet Marcos Ana, who spent twenty years in Franco's prisons. **9 May.** Press conference in Madrid to announce the beginning of shooting *Broken Embraces*, in Madrid and on Lanzarote, in the Canaries. Almodóvar announces a 'celebration of fiction' and kisses Lluís Homar on the mouth. **6 September.** End of the shoot, the longest of Almodóvar's career.

2009

13 February. Broadcast on Canal Plus Spain of *La Concejala antropófaga*, a short made on the set of *Broken Embraces*. **18 March.** Spanish release of *Broken Embraces*. The film is slated by Carlos Boyero, the new critic with *El País*. **19 May.** *Broken Embraces* is presented in competition at the Cannes Festival. **August.** Almodóvar engages in a dispute with the Vatican over the concept of the family, advising the Pope to 'get out and see ... that a family can consist of separated parents, cross-dressers or transsexuals.'

Penélope Cruz, Pedro Almodóvar and Carmen Maura at the 2006 Cannes Film Festival.

Filmography

SHORT FILMS

Dos putas o   1974
historia de amor que
termina in boda
Format Super 8.
Running time 10 mins.

La caída de Sodoma   1974
Format Super 8.
Running time 10 mins.

Film político   1974
Format Super 8.
Running time 4 mins.

Blancor   1975
Format Super 8.
Running time 5 mins.

Homenaje   1975
Format Super 8.
Running time 10 mins.

El sueño o la Estrella   1975
Format Super 8.
Running time 12 mins.

Muerte en   1976
la carretera
Format Super 8.
Running time 8 mins.
With Paloma Hurtado, Juan
Lombardero, Pepe Maya.

Sea caritativo   1976
Format Super 8.
Running time 5 mins.

Tráiler de '¿Quién   1976
teme a Virginia Woolf?'
Format Super 8.

Las tres ventajas   1977
de ponte
Format Super 8.

Sexo va, sexo viene   1977
Format Super 8.
Running time 17 mins.

Salomé   1978
Format 16mm.
Running time 12 mins.
With Isabel Mestres,
Fernando Hilbeck,
Agustín Almodóvar.

Tráiler para 'Amantes   1985
de lo prohibido'
Format 35mm.
Running time 20 mins.
With Bibí Andersen, Sonia
Hoffman, Josele Román.

La Concejala   2008
antropófaga
Format 35mm.
Running time 7 mins.
With Carmen Matchi,
Penélope Cruz, Marta Aledo.

FEATURE FILMS

Folle ... Folle...   1978
Fólleme Tim!
Screenplay Pedro Almodovar **For-**
mat Super 8. **Running time** 1h 30.
With Carmen Maura.

• A salesgirl at a department store
is engaged to a blind guitar-player.
He becomes famous and she in turn
loses her sight.

Pepi, Luci, Bom and   1980
Other Girls on the Heap
Pepi, Luci, Bom y
otras chicas del montón
Screenplay Pedro Almodóvar.
Cinematography Paco Femenia.
Sound Miguel Ángel Polo. **Edit-**
ing José Salcedo. **Music** Alaska
y Los Pegamoides. **Production**
Félix Rotaeta, Pepón Coromina for
Figaro Films. **Running time** 1h 20.
With Carmen Maura (Pepi), Olvido
'Alaska' Gara (Bom), Eva Siva (Luci),
Félix Rotaeta (The policeman), Kiti
Manver (The singer), Cecilia Roth
(The newscaster).

• Pepi is raped by a policeman, who
threatens to report her for growing cannabis on her windowsill. In
revenge, she throws Luci, the policeman's wife, into the arms of Bom, a
sadistic punk rock singer. Luci and
Bom have a passionate love affair,
Pepi becomes a designer in an
advertising agency that spends most
of its budget on promoting deodor-
izing underclothes. Luci is caught
by her husband, who beats her up,
which she loves. Pepi and Bom
decide to move in together.

Labyrinth of Passion   1982
Laberinto de pasiones
Screenplay Pedro Almodóvar. **Cin-**
ematography Ángel Luis Fernández.
Sound Martin Müller. **Produc-**
tion design Andrés Santana,
Pedro Almodóvar. **Editing** José
Salcedo. **Music** Almodóvar and
McNamara, various songs. **Pro-**
duction Alphaville. **Running time**
1h 40. With Cecilia Roth (Sexilia),
Imanol Arias (Riza Niro), Helga Liné
(Toraya), Marta Fernández Muro
(Queti), Fernando Vivanco (The

doctor), Fanny McNamara (Fabio),
Antonio Banderas (Sadeq), Agustín
Almodóvar (Hassan).

• Sexilia, a singer on the Madrid
underground rock scene, tries to
overcome her nymphomania. Riza,
son of the dethroned Emperor of
Tiran, cruises the Madrid streets for
boys and girls. Sadeq, who belongs
to an Islamist group tasked with
assassinating Riza, falls in love with
him, as does Sexilia. The singer
leaves her clothes at a dry cleaner's.
The owner has gone mad, and mis-
takes his daughter for his wife, forc-
ing her to do what he considers
her conjugal duty. To comfort herself in her misery, the dry cleaner's
daughter borrows Sexilia's clothes.
The Empress Toraya, Riza's mother,
tries to overcome her infertility and
give the Emperor an heir who is
worthy of him. To do this, she uses
the services of Sexilia's father, a
gynaecologist.

Dark Habits   1983
Entre tinieblas
Screenplay Pedro Almodóvar.
Cinematography Ángel Luis
Fernández. **Sound** Martin Müller,
Armin Fausten. **Production design**
Pin Morales, Román Arango. **Edit-**
ing José Salcedo. **Songs** Sol Pilas.
Production Tesauro SA. **Running**
time 1h 55. With Cristina S. Pascual
(Yolanda), Julieta Serrano (The
Mother Superior), Marisa Paredes
(Sister Manure), Carmen Maura
(Sister Damned), Chus Lampreave
(Sister Sewer Rat), Cecilia Roth.

• After accidentally causing her lover's death by overdose, the cabaret singer Yolanda seeks refuge in
a convent. The Mother Superior of
the Humiliated Sisters of Redemption has in fact visited her in her
dressing-room a short time previously. The community is made up
of half a dozen nuns, who include
a drug addict, a writer – under a
pseudonym – of pornographic novels, and one who keeps a tiger in
a cage. The owner of the convent,
a noblewoman, threatens to sell
it. Yolanda rejects the love of the
Mother Superior, who still continues to supply her with heroin, and
the community is unable to sur-
vive these crises. The nuns each
go their own way.

What Have I Done   1984
to Deserve This?
¿Qué he hecho yo
para merecer ésto?
Screenplay Pedro Almodóvar. **Cin-**
ematography Ángel Luis Fernández.
Sound Bernardo Menz. **Production**
design Pin Morales, Román Arango.
Costumes Cecilia Roth. **Editing**
José Salcedo. **Music** Bernardo
Bonezzi. **Production** Tesauro SA.
Running time 1h 42. With Carmen
Maura (Gloria), Ángel de Andrés
López (Antonio), Chus Lampreave
(The grandmother), Verónica Forqué
(Cristal), Kiti Manver (Juani).

• Gloria lives in a run-down high-rise
estate on the outskirts of Madrid
with her husband Antonio, a taxi
driver who carries a torch for a German singer whose driver and lover
he once was. They have two children, one a rent boy, the other a
drug addict. The grandmother who
lives with them dreams of returning
to her village. Gloria earns her living
by doing long hours of cleaning and
takes amphetamines to keep going.
When the woman at the pharmacy
refuses to renew her prescription,
and her husband gets involved in
an historical fraud for the sake of
the German singer, who has reap-
peared from the past, Gloria is completely out of her depth. Her neighbours, Cristal the prostitute and
Juani the model housewife, don't
give her much help.

Matador   1986
Screenplay Pedro Almodóvar
and Jesús Ferrero. **Cinematog-**
raphy Ángel Luis Fernández. **Sound**
Bernard Ortion. **Production design**
Román Arango, José Morales and
Josep Rosell. **Editing** José Salcedo.
Music Bernardo Bonezzi. **Produc-**
tion manager Esther García. **Pro-**
duction Andrés Vicente Gómez
for Compania Iberoamericana de
TV. **Running time** 1h 36. With
Assumpta Serna (María Cardenal),
Antonio Banderas (Ángel), Nacho
Martínez (Diego), Eva Cobo (Eva),
Julieta Serrano (Berta), Chus Lam-
preave (Pilar), Carmen Maura (Julia),

Eusebio Poncela (The commissaire), Bibí Andersen (The florist).

• Ángel, a very young man whose mind sometimes goes blank, is trying to become a bullfighter under instruction from Diego, a retired matador who has opened a school. One evening, to prove his virility, which is constantly put in question by his abusive mother who is a member of Opus Dei, Ángel rapes Eva, a young model who is Diego's mistress. Ángel hands himself in to the police and is defended by María Cardenal, a lawyer specializing in political trials, who is also a serial killer of her lovers, a trait she shares with Diego. The lawyer and the matador start a deadly liaison, and Ángel and Eva are drawn into its torments.

Law of Desire 1987
La ley del deseo
Screenplay Pedro Almodóvar. **Cinematography** Ángel Luis Fernández. **Sound** James Willis. **Production design** Javier Fernández. **Editing** José Salcedo. **Music** Bernardo Bonezzi, extracts from works by Shostakovich and Stravinsky. **Songs** Almodóvar and McNamara, Jacques Brel, Bola de Nieve. **Production manager** Esther García. **Production** Agustín Almodóvar for El Deseo. **Running time** 1h 40. With Eusebio Poncela (Pablo Quintero), Carmen Maura (Tina Quintero), Antonio Banderas (Antonio Benítez), Miguel Molina (Juan), Manuela Velasco (Ada), Bibí Andersen (Ada's mother), Victoria Abril (The girl in the night club).

• Pablo Quintero is a trendy film director whose boyfriend, Juan, goes away on holiday. Taking advantage of his absence, Antonio Benítez, a somewhat psychotic young man, insinuates himself into the director's life and murders Juan. Tina, Pablo's transsexual sister (she was born Tino) and her daughter Ada are in their turn threatened by Antonio.

Women on the Verge 1988
of a Nervous Breakdown
Mujeres al borde de un ataque de nervios

Screenplay Pedro Almodóvar. **Cinematography** José Luis Alcaine. **Sound** Gille Ortion. **Production design** Felix Murcia. **Editing** José Salcedo. **Music** Bernardo Bonezzi. **Songs** Lola Beltrán, La Lupe. **Production manager** Esther García. **Production** Agustín Almodóvar for El Deseo. **Running time** 1h 35. With Carmen Maura (Pepa), Julieta Serrano (Lucía), Antonio Banderas (Carlos), Fernando Guillén (Ivan), María Barranco (Candela), Rossy de Palma (Marisa), Kiti Manver (Paulina), Chus Lampreave (The concierge), Francesca Caballero (The announcer).

• Pepa has been abandoned by Ivan and wants to leave the flat in which they were lovers. But it becomes the place where several women meet: Candela, who is fleeing the police because she loved a terrorist, Lucía, the mother of one of Ivan's children, and Marisa, who has come to look at the flat with her partner, Carlos. All these women reach crisis point at the same moment, in the same place.

Tie Me Up! 1990
Tie Me Down!
¡Átame!
Screenplay Pedro Almodóvar. **Cinematography** José Luis Alcaine. **Production design** Ferrán Sánchez. **Editing** José Salcedo. **Music** Ennio Morricone. **Production manager** Esther García. **Production** Agustín Almodóvar for El Deseo. **Running time** 1h 41. With Victoria Abril (Marina), Antonio Banderas (Ricki), Francisco Rabal (Máximo Espejo), Loles León (Lola), Julieta Serrano (Alma), Rossy de Palma (The dealer on a scooter).

• Ricki, recently released from a psychiatric hospital, decides to take up again with Marina, with whom he slept once. Since then, she has become an actress, starting out in porn films. Ricki goes to the set where Marina, who is also a heroin addict, is filming under the direction of Máximo Espejo, a veteran Spanish filmmaker. Ricki kidnaps the young woman and forces her to have sex with him. Gradually, Marina gives in to the psychopath's sexual pressure.

High Heels 1991
Tacones lejanos
Screenplay Pedro Almodóvar. **Cinematography** Alfredo Mayo. **Sound** Jean-Paul Mugel. **Production design** Pierre-Louis Thévenet. **Editing** José Salcedo. **Music** Ryuichi Sakamoto. **Songs** Luz Casals. **Production manager** Esther García. **Production** Agustín Almodóvar for El Deseo, Ciby 2000. **Running time** 1h 53. With Victoria Abril (Rebeca), Marisa Paredes (Becky del Páramo), Miguel Bosé (The judge, Hugo, Letal), Feodor Atkine (Manuel).

• Abandoned by her mother (the singer Becky del Páramo, who has gone off to make a career in Mexico), Rebeca has become a TV news presenter. To make up for her mother's absence, she likes to watch the drag artist Letal, who impersonates Becky. Becky returns to Madrid and discovers that Rebeca is married to Manuel, her old lover. Soon he is murdered, and the judge in charge of the case has a strange resemblance to Letal. During the investigations, Rebeca is jailed on the evening of her mother's first concert.

Kika 1993
Screenplay Pedro Almodóvar. **Cinematography** Alfredo Mayo. **Sound** Jean-Paul Mugel. **Production design** Javier Fernández. **Costumes** Victoria Abril, Jean-Paul Gaultier. **Editing** José Salcedo. **Music** Bernard Hermann, Perez Prado, Chavela Vargas and others. **Production manager** Esther García. **Production** Agustín Almodóvar for El Deseo, Ciby 2000. **Running time** 1h 52. With Verónica Forqué (Kika), Victoria Abril (Andrea 'Scarface'), Peter Coyote (Nicholas), Álex Casanovas (Ramón), Rossy de Palma (Juana).

• Kika, a television make-up artist, is a gay woman who lives with Ramón, a sad man who has lost his mother. His American stepfather, Nicholas, was once Kika's lover. Ramón himself has had an affair with Andrea,

the presenter of a sleazy TV reality show. When Kika is raped by the brother of Juana, her cleaner, Andrea films it all.

The Flower of 1995
My Secret
La flor de mi secreto
Screenplay Pedro Almodóvar. **Cinematography** Affonso Beato. **Sound** Bernardo Menz. **Production design** Wolfgang Burmann, Miguel López Pelegrín. **Editing** José Salcedo. **Music** Alberto Iglesias. **Production manager** Esther García. **Production** Agustín Almodóvar for El Deseo, Ciby 2000. **Running time** 1h 42. With Marisa Paredes (Leo), Juan Echanove (Ángel), Imanol Arias (Paco), Rossy de Palma (Rosa), Chus Lampreave (Leo's mother).

• An author of romantic novels under the pseudonym Amanda Gris, Leo cannot own up to her success any more than she can admit that her marriage to Paco, an officer attached to Nato, is over. Her almost blind mother wants to leave Madrid to return to her village and Leo tries to start a new career, offering her services to *El País*. The first article she is asked to write is a review of a book by Amanda Gris. After a last attempt to regain her husband's love, she swallows half a tube of sleeping pills.

Live Flesh 1997
Carne tremula
Screenplay Pedro Almodóvar, Ray Lorriga, Jorge Guerricaechevarría, based on Ruth Rendell's novel, *Live Flesh*. **Cinematography** Affonso Beato. **Sound** Bernardo Menz. **Production design** Antxón Gómez. **Editing** José Salcedo. **Music** Alberto Iglesias. **Production manager** Esther García. **Production** Agustín Almodóvar for El Deseo, Ciby 2000. **Running time** 1h 39. With Javier Bardem (David), Francesca Neri (Helena), Liberto Rabal (Victor), Ángela Molina (Clara), Penélope Cruz (Isabel).

• Victor is born on a Madrid bus, on the night when a state of emergency is declared. Twenty years later, he is caught in an exchange of fire which involves two police officers, David and Sancho, and a girl, Helena. Victor is convicted of having fired the gun and is sent to prison. David, who is now paralysed, moves in with Helena. On his release from prison, Victor tries to win her back by seducing Clara, Sancho's wife.

All About My Mother   1999
Todo sobre mi madre
Screenplay Pedro Almodóvar. **Cinematography** Affonso Beato. **Sound** Miguel Rejas. **Production design** Antxón Gómez. **Editing** José Salcedo. **Music** Alberto Iglesias. **Production manager** Esther García. **Production** Agustín Almodóvar for El Deseo, Renn Productions. **Running time** 1h 40. With Cecilia Roth (Manuela), Marisa Paredes (Huma Rojo), Penélope Cruz (Rosa).
• Manuela lives alone with her son Esteban, whom she worships. To celebrate his seventeenth birthday, she takes him to the theatre to see the great actress Huma Rojo in *A Streetcar Named Desire*. When they come out, Esteban asks Huma for her autograph, and he is knocked down and killed by a car. Manuela, who had promised her son she would tell him who his father was, goes off in search of him.

Talk to Her   2002
Hable con ella
Screenplay Pedro Almodóvar. **Cinematography** Javier Aguirresarobe. **Sound** Miguel Rejas. **Production design** Antxón Gómez. **Choreography** Pina Bausch. **Editing** José Salcedo. **Music** Alberto Iglesias. **Songs** Caetano Veloso. **Production manager** Esther García. **Production** Agustín Almodóvar for El Deseo. **Running time** 1h 52. With Javier Cámara (Benigno), Dario Grandinetti (Marco), Leonor Watling (Alicia), Rosario Flores (Lydia), Geraldine Chaplin (Katerina Bilova).
• Some time after they found themselves sitting next to each other at a performance by Pina Bausch, Benigno and Marco meet at a clinic.

Benigno is a nurse, looking after a young dancer, Alicia, who is in a coma. Marco sits with his partner, Lydia, a bullfighter who is also unconscious after being gored. While Marco gradually grows apart from Lydia, Benigno is increasingly attracted to Alicia. He rapes her and she becomes pregnant by him. When this comes to light, he is prosecuted and sentenced.

Bad Education   2004
La mala educación
Screenplay Pedro Almodóvar. **Cinematography** José Luis Alcaine. **Sound** Miguel Rejas. **Production design** Antxón Gómez. **Editing** José Salcedo. **Music** Alberto Iglesias. **Production manager** Esther García. **Production** Agustín Almodóvar for El Deseo. **Running time** 1h 45. With Gael García Bernal (Ángel), Fele Martínez (Enrique Goded), Javier Cámara (Paquito).
• Enrique Goded, a film director, receives a visit one day from an actor whose stage name is Ángel and who insists he is Ignacio, Enrique's first love when the two boys were both boarders at a religious school. Enrique was expelled by Father Manolo, the school's Father Superior, and Ángel-Ignacio offers the director a screenplay that relates the circumstances in which Father Manolo abused him. Enrique is attracted by the project but feels increasingly uneasy with Ángel, who demands the leading role in the film.

Volver   2006
Screenplay Pedro Almodóvar. **Cinematography** José Luis Alcaine. **Sound** Miguel Rejas. **Production design** Salvador Parra. **Editing** José Salcedo. **Music** Alberto Iglesias. **Production manager** Esther García. **Production** Agustín Almodóvar for El Deseo. **Running time** 2h. With Penélope Cruz (Raimunda), Carmen Maura (Irene), Lola Dueñas (Sole), Yohana Cobo (Paula), Chus Lampreave (Tía Paula).
• In a windswept village in La Mancha, Raimunda, her daughter Paula and her sister Sole are cleaning the family

graves in the cemetery. Their mother Irene died in a fire, and there are rumours in the village that the old woman regularly appears in the family house, where Aunt Paula lives. On her return to Madrid, Paula kills her father, who was trying to rape her. Raimunda hides the body and sets out to make a new life shared between her city neighbourhood and her village.

Broken Embraces   2009
Los abrazos rotos
Screenplay Pedro Almodóvar. **Cinematography** Rodrigo Prieto. **Sound** Miguel Rejas. **Production design** Antxón Gómez. **Editing** José Salcedo. **Music** Alberto Iglesias. **Production manager** Esther García. **Production** Agustín Almodóvar for El Deseo. **Running time** 2h 09. With Penélope Cruz (Lena), Lluis Homar (Mateo Blanco/Harry Caine), Blanca Portillo (Judit), José Luis Gómez (Ernesto Martel), Ruben Ochandiano (Ray X), Tamar Novas (Diego), Ángela Molina (The mother of Lena), Chus Lampreave (The concierge), Rossy De Palma (Julieta).
• Harry Caine is a blind screenwriter who has given up his own name. In the days when he was called Mateo Blanco and could see, he was a director. He had had an intense affair with Lena, a young woman who had become an actress with the help of her rich lover and former boss, Ernesto Martel, a figure from the Spanish financial boom of the 1980s. But for a filmmaker, a liaison with his producer's mistress is a recipe for disaster. Twenty-five years later, Mateo/Harry's past is still coming to the surface.

PRODUCER ONLY

Pestañas postizas   1982
by Enrique Belloch
Acción Mutante   1993
by Álex de la Iglesia
Mi nombre es sombra 1996
by González Suárez
Shampoo Horns   1998
by Manuel Toledano
The Devil's Backbone 2001
El espinazo del diablo
by Guillermo del Toro
My Life Without Me   2003
Mi vida sin mí
by Isabel Coïxet
Chill Out!   2003
Descongélate
by Dunia Ayaso and
Felix Sabroso
The Holy Girl   2004
La niña santa
by Lucrecia Martel
The Secret Life   2005
of Words
La vida secreta
de las palabras
by Isabel Coïxet
The Headless Woman 2008
La mujer sin cabeza
by Lucrecia Martel

Selected Bibliography

Mark Allinson,
*A Spanish Labyrinth:
The Films of Pedro Almodóvar,*
I B Tauris & Co Ltd, London, 2001.

Pedro Almodóvar,
Patti Diphusa and Other Writings,
Faber and Faber, New York, 1999.

Pedro Almodóvar: Interviews,
University Press of Mississippi,
Jackson, 2004.

Marvin D'Lugo,
Pedro Almodóvar,
University of Illinois Press, 2006.

Brad Epps & Despina Kakoudaki,
*All about Almodóvar: a passion
for cinema,*
University of Minnesota Press,
2009.

Frederic Strauss,
Almodóvar on Almodóvar,
Faber and Faber, London, 1996.

Sources

Collection Pedro Almodóvar: p.2, 6, 7, 8–9, 11, 25, 74–5, 79, 98, 99 (1st col.).
Collection Cahiers du cinéma: 4–5, 16–7, 18, 20, 21, 22–3, 24, 26–7, 28, 30, 31, 32, 34–5, 40, 41, 42–3, 44, 46 (bottom), 46–7, 48, 49, 50–1, 52, 53, 58–9, 62–3, 66–7, 78, 80–1, 82–3, 84, 85, 86–7, 88–9, 90, 91, 99 (2nd col.), 100, 101 (1st col. top; 2nd col.; 3rd col. bottom; 4th col.), 102 (1st col. bottom; 2nd col.).
Collection CAT'S: p.38–9, 76–7, 101 (1st col. bottom).
El Deseo: p.12, 14–5, 29, 36, 45, 54, 55, 72–3, 101 (3rd col. top), 102 (1st col. top).
Pathé Distribution: p. 92–3, 94, 95, 96–7, 102 (3rd col.), 104.
Screen grabs: p.68.

Credits

© Pedro Almodóvar: p.2, 6, 7, 8–9, 11, 25, 98.
© Catherine Cabrol: p.74–5, 99 (1st col.).
© Ceesepe: p. 14–5.
© El Deseo: p.12, 16–7, 29, 65 (bottom), 68, 85, 92–3, 94, 95, 96–7, 100 (1st col. top), 102 (3rd col.), 104.
© El Deseo/José Luis Alcaine: Cover, 32 (left), 80–1, 82–3, 84, 102 (2nd col. top).
© El Deseo/Jorge Aparicio: p.18, 20, 21, 22–3, 30, 31, 32 (right), 34–5, 100 (1st col. bottom), 100 (3rd col.), 101 (1st col. top).
© El Deseo/Paula Ardizzoni / Emilio Pereda: p.86–7, 88–9, 90, 91, 92–3, 94, 95, 96–7, 102 (2nd col. bottom; 3rd col.), 104.
© El Deseo/Antonio de Benito: p.26–7, 28, 100 (2nd col. bottom).
© El Deseo/Miguel Bracho: p.76–7, 78, 102 (1st col. bottom).
© El Deseo/Mimmo Cattarinich: p.44, 46 (bottom), 46–7, 48, 49, 50–1, 52, 53, 99 (2nd col.), 101 (2nd col.).
© El Deseo/Macusa Cores: p.38–9, 40, 42–3, 101 (1st col. bottom).
© El Deseo/Teresa Isasi: p.4–5, 66–7, 69, 70–1, 71 (bottom), 72–3, 102 (1st col. top).
© El Deseo/Jean-Marie Leroy: p.54, 55, 56–7, 60, 61, 64, 65, 69, 70–1, 71 (bottom), 56–7, 58–9, 60, 61, 101 (3rd col.).
© El Deseo/Daniel Martinez: p.62–3, 64, 65 (top), 101 (4th col.).
© El Deseo/Ana Muller: p.24, 45, 100 (2nd col. top).
© Brigitte Lacombe: cover.
© Paco Navarro: p.36, 41.
© Traverso: p.99 (4th col.).

All reasonable efforts have been made to trace the copyright holders of the photographs used in this book. We apologize to anyone that we were unable to reach.

Cover: Pedro Almodóvar photographed by Catherine Lacombe in 2002.
Inside front cover: Pedro Almodóvar on the set of *Bad Education* (2004).
Inside back cover: Penélope Cruz and Pedro Almodóvar on the set of *Broken Embraces* (2009).

Cahiers du cinéma Sarl
65, rue Montmartre
75002 Paris

www.cahiersducinema.com

Revised English Edition © 2010 Cahiers du cinéma Sarl
First published in French as *Pedro Almodóvar* © 2007 Cahiers du cinéma Sarl

ISBN 978 2 8664 2567 8

Series conceived by Claudine Paquot
Designed by Werner Jeker/Les Ateliers du Nord
Translated by Imogen Forster
Printed in China